Sample Paper for Exam Success

Information Technology

for Class IX

(As per the CBSE Syllabus Code 402)

Komalpreet Kaur

Dr. Yogesh Kumar

www.bpbonline.com

FIRST EDITION 2021
REPRINT 2024

ISBN: 978-93-90684-33-5

Distributors:

BPB PUBLICATIONS
20, Ansari Road, Darya Ganj
New Delhi-110002
Ph: 23254990/23254991

DECCAN AGENCIES
4-3-329, Bank Street,
Hyderabad-500195
Ph: 24756967/24756400

MICRO MEDIA
Shop No. 5, Mahendra Chambers,
150 DN Rd. Next to Capital Cinema,
V.T. (C.S.T.) Station, MUMBAI-400 001
Ph: 22078296/22078297

BPB BOOK CENTRE
376 Old Lajpat Rai Market,
Delhi-110006
Ph: 23861747

To View Complete
BPB Publications Catalogue
Scan the QR Code:

Published by Manish Jain for BPB Publications, 20 Ansari Road, Darya Ganj, New Delhi-110002 and Printed by him at Manipal Technologies Limited, Manipal

www.bpbonline.com

About the Author

Komalpreet Kaur has good experience in writing research documents of Computer and Electronics. She has done her Masters in Technology in Electronics and Communication and have 3 years of experience in Research and IT field. She is also pursuing her Ph.D. from Punjabi University, Patiala.
LinkedIn: *linkedin.com/in/komalpreet-kaur-9a9b6946*

Dr. Yogesh Kumar is working as Associate Professor at Chandigarh Group of Colleges, Landran, Mohali. He has done his Ph.D, M.Tech in computer science from Punjabi University, Patiala. He is having total 13 years of experience including teaching and research. His research areas include Natural Language Processing, Computer Vision, Machine Learning and Data Science.
LinkedIn: *linkedin.com/in/yogesh-kumar-819a5275*

Preface

With the recent revision of the syllabus for Information Technology, the CBSE has changed the marking scheme and the exam pattern. All this has been kept in mind while writing this sample paper. The book in your hand is strictly based on the new CBSE syllabus and promises to deliver the content keeping in mind the learning objectives of the computer science subject.

The papers are divided into four sections.

- **Section A** contains multiple choice questions of 1 mark each. You have to attempt any of 6 questions from this section.
- **Section B** consists of very short questions of 2 marks each. You have to attempt all the questions.
- **Section C** consists of short questions of 3 marks each.
- **Section D** consists of long questions of 5 marks each.

For each chapter Knowledge tip, Tech tip, Mind map and Exam tips has been given. It will help you to prepare for the examination as the ten solved papers and five unsolved are provided with solutions and marking schemes as per CBSE. It covers the questions which are asked in exams and will help you to achieve good grades.

Table of Contents

Extra Bytes

1 CHAPTER Introduction to IT and ITeS Industry

■ KNOWLEDGE TIPS

- Information and Communication Technology includes a set of technological resources and tools used for communication, creation, storing, managing, and disseminating information.
- IT is a study, design, development, implementation, storing, support, and management of all computer-based information systems, particularly software applications and computer hardware.
- Some of the benefits of business is to improve efficiency, increase profit, minimize waste, reduce cost, provide better service to customers, and many more.
- ITeS is an abbreviation for information technology-enabled services and also known as web-enabled services or teleworking that defined as outsourcing of processes that enabled with information technology and covered diverse areas like HR, healthcare, finance, administration, manufacturing, telecommunication, and more.
- BPO Business Process Outsourcing services that are meant to perform business operations through an outside service provider. BPM stands for Business Process Management that defines how a company creates, edits, and analyses the predictable processes that make up the core of its business.
- Some of the factors that have influenced the Indian IT-BPM industry till the year are revamped partnership, disruptive technology, and enhancement of skillsets.
- A multinational company is a business that operates in many different countries at the same time. Indian Service Providers companies are started with their operations in India, and most of these organizations have their headquarters in India, but their offices can be in many international locations.
- Global In-house centers organizations gratify only the needs of their parent company and do not serve external clients. Information technology or IT is the use of any computers, storage, networking, and other physical devices or processes for creating, processing, exchanging, and storing all forms of electronic data.
- Various application areas of IT are home computing, library, workplace, education, entertainment, communication, business, science and engineering, banking, insurance, marketing, health, and agriculture.
- For working at homes, a personal computer or PC is used for performing household work. Libraries are the main information center that has also started using IT and computers for the benefit of mankind as a whole. In workplaces or offices, computers and their applications are used to perform work more effectively that makes computer use as prevalent.

- The information technology and the Internet have become a major source of entertainment. Computers are also being used by scientists and engineers for performing complex scientific calculations and drawing, designing, and testing or simulation of design.
- IT also helps the banking industry to deal with the challenges poses by the new economy. Insurance companies also use computers to create a database that contains all records up to date. IT in marketing is used for planning, managing, and monitoring campaigns a computer technology and is used by marketing professions.
- Information technology in Healthcare is a broad term that describes the technology and infrastructure used for recording, analysing, and sharing patient health data.

■ TECH TIPS

- **Information Technology (IT):** IT is a study, design, development, implementation, storing, support, and management of all computer-based information systems, particularly software applications and computer hardware.
- **Technology:** Technology means the use of hardware, software, services, and supporting infrastructure to manage and deliver information using voice, data, and video.
- **ITeS:** ITeS means information technology-enabled services and also known as web-enabled services or teleworking that defined as outsourcing of processes that enabled with information technology and covered diverse areas like HR, healthcare, finance, administration, manufacturing, telecommunication, and many more.
- **BPO:** BPO stands for Business Process Outsourcing services that are meant to perform business operations through an outside service provider.
- **BPM:** BPM stands for Business Process Management that defines how a company creates, edits, and analyses the predictable processes that make up the core of its business.
- **Integration-centric BPM:** It handles the processes of primarily jumping between HRMS, CRM like existing systems with much involvement of humans.
- **Human-centric BPM:** These are for humans executed processes. In this, a lot of approvals and tasks are performed by individuals.
- **Document-centric BPM:** These are required when document like an agreement is the main part of the process. They enable verifying, routing, getting, and formatting the document signed as the tasks pass along the workflow.
- **Multinational companies (MNCs):** A multinational company is a business that operates in many different countries at the same time. Mainly their headquarters are outside India, but it is operated in multiple locations worldwide. They handle both domestic and global clients.
- **Indian Service Providers (ISPs):** These companies are started with their operations in India, and most of these organizations have their headquarters in India, but their offices can be in many international locations. They handle both global and domestic clients, but some of the ISP's companies serve only Indian clients.

- **Global In-house Centers (GIC):** These organizations gratify only the needs of their parent company and do not serve external clients. Or we can also say that these organizations are offshore centers that perform designated functions for large organizations. This allows the organization to keep IT operations in-house and expand its global footprint by offering opportunities for innovation in a cost-effective manner.
- **Libraries:** Libraries are the main information center that has also started using IT and computers for the benefit of mankind as a whole.
- **IT at Workplace:** Technology is such an integral part of the 21st century workplace that any business without some level of technical knowledge will fail. In workplaces or offices, computers and their applications are used to perform work more effectively that makes computer use as prevalent. Some offices or companies may find functioning without them is virtually impossible.
- **IT in Education:** Education and learning are lifetime processes that don't have any limit to start and stop. The speed of information delivery has been increased by information technology that results in the improvement of the education environment. Nowadays, computers and information technology are used in education for teaching, learning, and assessment.
- **Teaching aids and media:** Information technology and computer makes it easy to access academic information at any time. Both students and teachers use information technology for acquiring and exchanging educational material.
- **IT in Entertainment:** Advancement in technology helps in improving every aspect of the home environment, including home entertainment systems. IT and the internet is a major source of entertainment. When we go back in years, then there were limited options for enjoying entertainment at home. However, this has been changed by the invention of cable and satellite TV as people are able to access a range of channels.
- **IT in communication:** The use of technology in communication has become a necessity; it's now become a part of our lives. The advancement in technology has made a great impact on the way we communicate. Over the years, communication methods have evolved from simple text messages and audio calls to more efficient video calls and chat platforms that offer other communication services.
- **IT in business:** Information technology drives innovation, and innovation is the path to business success. IT has become very important in the business world from your company's online store to enterprise software; there is a need to record the transactions and gather information. In every business organization, computers are used for payroll calculation, sales analysis, managing stocks, financial forecasting, budgeting, and maintaining stocks.
- **IT in banking:** IT also helps the banking industry to deal with the challenges poses by the new economy. To meet the needs of customers, financial institutions rely on gathering, processing, analyzing, and providing information. For the banking industry, a new service, new products, efficient delivery channels are opened by technology. Some of the examples of technology in banking are online electronics banking, internet banking, and mobile banking.
- **IT in insurance:** Insurance companies also use computers to create a database that contains all records up to date. The demand for new insurance products is ever-growing from traditional life and health insurance to ensure against natural disasters and cyberattacks. The insurance

companies keep the data of their policies, starting date, date of next installment, maturity date, interest dues, survival benefits, and bonus are declared using computers in insurance companies.

- **IT in healthcare:** Information technology in healthcare is a broad term that describes the technology and infrastructure used for recording, analyzing, and sharing patient health data.
- **Magnetic Resonance Imaging (MRI) machine:** MRI is a radiology technique scan that uses magnetism, radio waves, and computers to produce images of internal organs or structures. The digital images are very helpful in the detection of tiny changes within the body and also help in the detection of diseases and its treatment.
- **Cardiac screening machine:** Screening tests are used for finding the disease before symptoms begin, and the goal of screening is to detect disease at its earliest stage. The cardiac screening machine is used to displays the physiology of the heart and its inside movements. This machine is mainly used for diagnosis the problems related to heart like thinning of veins and then according to that recommend the treatment.
- **Computerized Axial Tomography (CAT) machine:** It uses a computer which is linked to an X-ray machine that makes a series of detailed pictures of areas inside the body. These pictures are taken from different angles and used to create 3-dimensional (3-D) views of tissues and organs. These images are helpful in the diagnosis of disease, its treatment, or find out how well the treatment is working.
- **Electrocardiogram (ECG) machine:** The ECG is a diagnostic tool that is routinely used to assess the electrical and muscular functions of the heart. This machine monitors the heartbeat and detects electrical impulses produced when blood is pumped by the heart to different parts of the body. Then the recorded electrical impulses by machine are shown in the form of a graph. In the case of interrupted or misguided electrical activities, there are chances of heart diseases.
- **Electroencephalography (EEG) machine:** EEG is a test used to evaluate the electrical activity in the brain. Brain cells communicate with each other through electrical impulses. The potential problems associated with this activity can be detected by this machine. It also records and tracks the patterns of brain waves. The small electrical probes are attached to the head for receiving the electrical impulses of the brain and send signals to a computer for recording the results.
- **Blood pressure measuring machine:** Device is worn on a wrist band for measuring the blood pressure of a person at rest or when a patient is involved in some physical activity. Now one can also monitor blood pressure at home by using digital blood pressure machines.
- **Blood sugar testing machine:** Device is used to analyze a blood glucose level in the body. For this purpose, a sample of blood is taken then put on a device that gives the level of blood glucose in the body. Now one can also monitor the blood sugar level at home by using digital blood sugar testing machines.

- **IT in everyday life:** Over the past few decades, it is a recognized fact that the application of IT in our daily life has changed dramatically. IT is used in every sphere of life like microwave oven, washing machines, OTG, television, printers, refrigerators, and many more products using which have embedded software in it.

■ MIND MAP

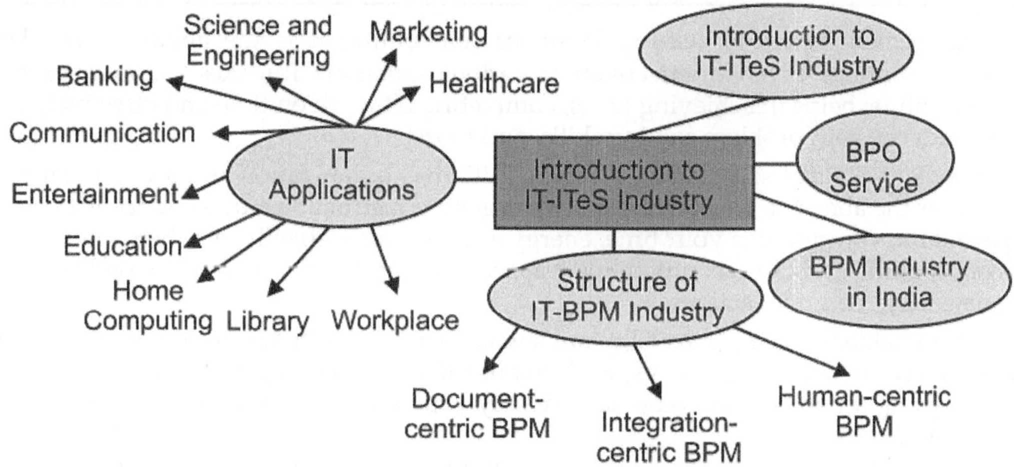

■ EXAM TIPS

1. Take a survey on various types of BPO services that helps in memorising it.
2. Ask question to any of your known person who work in IT industry to know various areas of application.
3. Check for different types of companies in your city and divide them according to the range.
4. Make a list of various ways of using ICT in the classroom.

2 CHAPTER Self-Management Skills

■ KNOWLEDGE TIPS

- Self-management refers to self-regulation or self-control; it is the ability to regulate one's thoughts, emotions, behavior effectively in various situations. It makes you more organized, in stills discipline, helps in achieving goals, completing all work on time and effectively, enhances self-confidence gain problem solving skills, and more.
- The three key-skills of self-management are initiative, organization and accountability. Where, initiative is the ability to work without always getting instructions for what needs to be done. By organization, you can plan your time, energy and resources effectively when you are organized in work and life and the accountability is specific to one's self in which one will be responsible for answering their own actions.
- Both accountability and responsibility are similar but have different meaning. As one can share responsibility but accountability is specific to oneself. In case of responsibility one can blame other for any wrong actions but in accountability only you will be responsible and have to answer for your actions.
- To achieve a bigger task or goal, you need to divide it into smaller parts and define your targets using SMART strategy. In SMART strategy, S stands for specific, M stands for Measurable (divide your tasks whose completion gives measurable outcome), A stands for Achievable (means set a task that can be achieved), R stands for Realistic, and T stands for Time bound.
- Self-management is important in every field of life as it teaches to be productively and efficiently achieve your goals. It also helps in managing time and completing tasks with less effort, managing stress, and prioritizing our tasks.
- Self-confidence is a sense of trusting one's own abilities and self. Social, cultural, and physical factors influence self-confidence. Building self-confidence is the process that takes efforts and commitment and it having a positive attitude about one's self.
- Social factor influencing self-management is Society that consists of school, friends, family and neighborhood, plays an important role in building and shaping our self-confidence. A long lasting impact is left on our outlook and attitude towards ourselves. How one perceives their self, gets affected by evaluation from teachers, friends, schoolmates, parents, etc.
- In cultural factors, Culture or characteristics of a community, society or group is reflected in its beliefs and practices. It includes culture behaviour and development and children growing up in different cultures receive specific inputs from their environment.
- In physical factors, to develop selfconfidence in people an important role is played by healthy mind, healthy physique and good appearance. Person's selfconfidence gets affected by the way they appear, in every culture. Behavior, body language and way of speaking reflect the level of confidence.
- Self-efficiency, positive thinking, self-esteem, locus of control, selfmanagement, experience, etc. are factors that build self-confidence.

- SWOT stands for Strength, Weakness, Opportunity, and Threat and it is a useful technique for understanding opportunities and challenges.

■ TECH TIPS

- **Communication:** Communication is a process of sharing information between two or multiple persons. There are number of ways to communicate written, visually, vocally, and nonverbally.
- **Sender:** Sender is the source who sends information or message. A sender can be a single person or a group of person who send information and message through an appropriate channel.
- **Encoding:** Encoding or converting data or information into the coded language that is not understood by any other person. It can be encoded by selecting specific alphabet, words or symbols that are clear to both sender and receiver.
- **Receiver:** Receiver is the person or group of person who will receive the sent information or message by sender and understand it by decoding it.
- **Communication channel:** The communication channel is the source through which data or information is sent from sender to receiver. An appropriate channel or medium is selected by the sender to send a message. The communication channel can be faxed, electronic mail, letters, face-to-face, telephone calls, and more.
- **Decoding:** The decoding is the opposite process of encoding in which the information or data in coded language is converted into original information. The encoded information is decoded at the receiver side to understand the sent message or information. The messages should be decoded according to the pattern used by the receiver while encoding it helps in having correct information.
- **Feedback:** Feedback is the response given to sender information. To complete the communication cycle, a feedback should be given by the receiver.
- **Oral communication:** Oral communication is the way of expressing ideas and information through spoken words and considered as a more natural form of communication as compared to written form due to immediate clarification and feedback is involved in it.
- **Written communication:** Written communication is the way of sharing information or ideas using written messages and it is considered as a most formal way of communication. While using written communication, people should have to choose words carefully, and its placement should be in order.
- **Non-verbal communication:** Non-verbal communication is the communication method in which information is exchanged using all other things except word. As it includes gestures, postures, eye contact, facial expressions, fingers and various other body and oral communication is supported in it.
- **Visual communication:** The visual communication is the method that relies on pictures, illusions, and graphics for sharing messages. A sense of sight used in any verbal and non-verbal communication is visual communication.
- **Perspective:** Perspective is the point of view of an individual through which one understands every communication and event happening around us. Everyone has different ways of seeing everything due to which everyone has different perspectives.
- **Visual Perspective:** Visual perspective is a mental block that comes from your own visual perception of something.
- **Prejudices:** Prejudices are prejudgment that is not based on experience, logic, or any fact. If sender or receiver have prejudices in their mind that it can result in communication failure

- **Attitude:** It is the mindset of one individual in taking a decision or responding to the same situation.
- **Sentence:** A group of words that make complete sense.
- **Asserted or declarative sentence:** The sentence that reports events, describe things and state facts. It is a simple sentence that indicates, declares or asserts, which gives positive or negative meaning.
- **Interrogative sentence:** These sentences are used to make enquiries and asking for information. At the end question mark is used and it starts with words like Why, What, When, How, and many more.
- **Imperative sentence:** These are the sentences that express an order, advice, request, suggestion, direction, etc. It ends with a full stop or explanation sign.
- **Exclamatory sentence:** These sentences express wonder, surprise, happiness, sorrow, sympathy or gratitude like strong and sudden feelings. It can form by either selecting how, what like words or oh, ah, hurrah, alas, oops like interjections.
- **Articles:** An article is a word used before a noun (person, object, place or idea). In the English language, there is a definite and indefinite article. 'A' and 'an' are Indefinite articles 'the' is a definite article.
- **Indefinite articles:** Indefinite articles are 'A' and 'An'. These articles are used before Singular Countable Nouns (SCN) that indicates a noun is not referring to any particular thing or person.
- **Definite articles:** 'The' is a definite article used with a plural uncountable noun and singular countable noun. It mainly used in specifying thing, place, and person.
- **Paragraph:** Paragraph is a number of related sentences focused on an idea. It forms a part of a larger piece of writing, such as a composition. The communication of idea in efficient and clear way is the basic aim of a paragraph that mainly discusses one aspect of the topic or subject.

■ MIND MAP

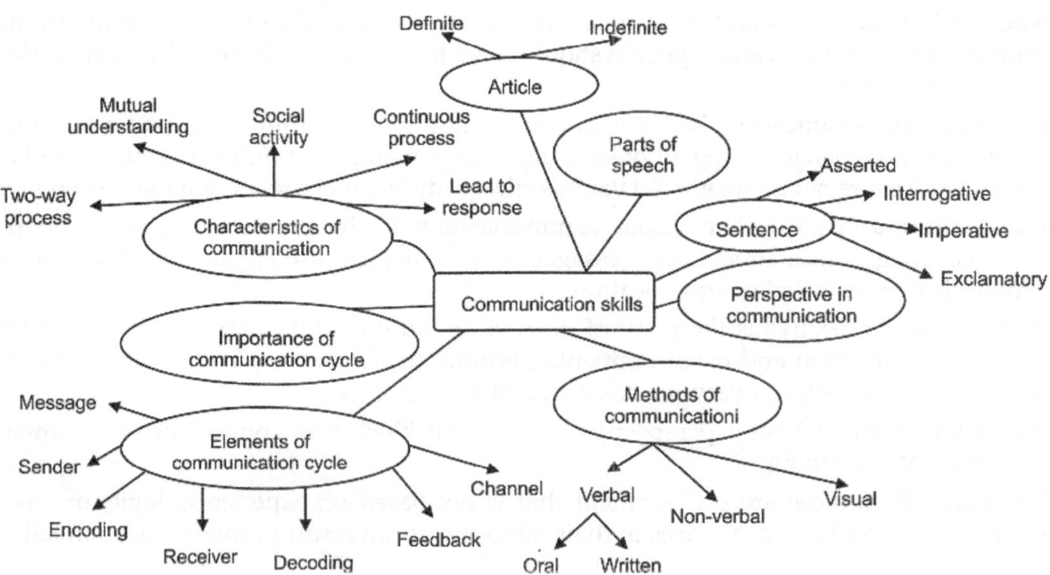

■ EXAM TIPS

1. Relate everything with your day to day life to keep things in mind for long time.
2. More Workout on practical work.

DATA ENTRY AND KEYBOARDING SKILLS

■ KNOWLEDGE TIPS

- The keyboard is an input device used to enter characters and functions into the computer system. The keyboard is a primary device with more than 100 keys used to enter text, and each key corresponds to a single symbol.
- Types of keys in Keyboard are Alphabetic keys, Alt key, Arrow key, Caps lock key, Delete key, Enter key or Return key, Esc key, Function keys, Home key, Insert key, Numlock key, Page up key, Page down key, Punctuation keys, Spacebar, Tab key and Shift or Alt keys.
- Sometimes the numeric keypad is a separate device but not built into a keyboard. This keyboard is usually connected to a computer with either a USB cable or serial connector.
- The home keys are the row of keys on the computer keyboard; on which your fingers rest on when not typing. The Alphabets ASDF are home keys for left hand and LKJ along with semi-colon (;) are for a right hand.
- For both hands, the thumb rests on the spacebar. The guide keys are those keys that help in moving the cursor using the keyboard.
- Typing ergonomics is used to reduce the stress, strain, wear and tear of your joints as you repeatedly type away. Keep your feet flat on the floor, and you can also use a footstool if required.
- Your mouse and keyboard should be near to each other around in the distance of 20 cms that helps in operating the keyboard smoothly and effortlessly. Do not bend your neck while working on the monitor, as bending forward will create too much pressure on your discs.
- From the floor, the height of the under-desk keyboard drawer or table top must be 68 to 73 cm. The writing matter must be kept either to the left side or right side of the keyboard or on anything that has a sloping surface.
- The correct position of fingers comes with mastery typewriting skills or attaining the necessary knowledge and skill of keyboard.
- During the keyboard operation in a home row or horizontal approach, all the eight fingers of both the hands rest on Home keys F, D, S, A, and J, K, L. Left-hand fingers must be placed on F, D, S, A, and right-hand fingers on J, K, L.
- To operate the second row, you have to place your fingers of each hand on the allotted keys. Now you will be left with key g and h that is operated by the forefingers of the left and right hand, respectively.

- To operate or press any key on the third or upper row, you have to take your finger from a to q by little left-hand finger and from ;) top by the little right hand finger.
- The mouse is a pointing device that consists of two or three buttons. One button is present on the left side, one on the right side and one in the middle. Various types of the mouse are mechanical mouse, opto-mechanical mouse, and optical mouse.
- The mouse pointer is also known as mouse arrow, mouse cursor is a graphical image that is used to control or activate certain elements in a graphical user interface.
- In the most common type of mouse, there are either two or three buttons on its top that are used for different actions. Some actions of the mouse are left click, Double click, right-click, scroll and drag and drop. Then right-click anywhere in the interface will display a context-sensitive menu or displays a set of commands and available options.
- The scroll wheel or wheel mouse is a rubber or plastic wheel located between the left and right buttons. The drag and drop action of mouse will help in selecting then moving the item or document from one location to another without using cut and paste feature.
- Rapid Typing Tutor is a free and open-source software that is designed for learning typing skills on the computer. The progress results are displayed after every lesson. You can use the statistics window to view the results of the already completed lessons.
- The title bar consists of program modes, option buttons, and three control buttons. The virtual keyboard is the keyboard of Rapid Typing software that helps the user to learn touch typing with all your fingers.
- On the extreme right side, there are three control buttons Minimize, Maximize, and Close button that is used to reduce the size of RapidTyping window, maximize the size, and to close the window, respectively.
- Text area or text panel is an area where the user sees the text typed by them. The status bar is present on the bottom of the text area that consists of tips, progress bars, and volume control.
- The user has to click on the current lesson tab given on the top left corner of the title bar. From drop-down arrow of course and lesson given below the title bar, the user can choose the required one.
- You can use the Statistics window to view the results of the already completed lessons. After completion of course interpretation of results is necessary to know your overall performance.
- In the statistics window, the red color indicates the wrong inputs within the acceptable timeframe. The green color indicates the right inputs, the yellow color indicates the right inputs exceeding the acceptable timeframe and the orange color indicates the wrong inputs that exceed the acceptable timeframe.
- Users can start the same lesson again if the better score is not achieved by them, or they can click on the next step tab to go on the next lesson. The detailed statistics for the current lesson can be seen on the error tab that shows your errors and delays percentage both in the table and graphical view.
- The detailed lesson statistics display the details like typing speed, errors, and slowdown for each chapter. On the left side of the title bar, there is a button of Lesson editor after the student statistics. By clicking on the lesson editor button, a lesson editor window will appear.

- The lesson editor window allows us to customize lessons that means you can add, change, import/export, and remove lessons and courses.
- In Rapid typing software, you can create a new lesson, delete a lesson. Editor panel is the area where changes can be done in existing course options or text of a lesson such as a navigation tree.
- You can delete the lesson by simply selecting it from the navigation tree and click on the delete button given on the toolbar.
- To create a new course, Select Lesson editor options; given on the title bar and select Create a new course from the Course menu option.
- To delete a newly created course, select the course and click on the delete button, or press delete key given on the keyboard.
- The typing speed can be measured with different accuracies. Typing accuracy is defined as the percentage of correct entries out of total entries typed.

■ TECH TIPS

- **Keyboard:** The keyboard is the piece of computer hardware used to input text, characters, and other commands into a computer or similar device.
- **Alphabetic keys:** There are 26 alphabets keys on the keyboard from A to Z. But these keys are not present in the alphabetic order. You can use these keys for typing words, sentences, or paragraphs.
- **Alt key:** Alt key stands for Alternate Keys that is press together with another Key so that the other key does something different from what it usually does. It is like a second control key.
- **Arrow keys:** There are four arrow keys for moving the cursor up, down, left, or right, and these are used for moving the cursor in the respective direction.
- **Backspace key:** Backspace key is similar to delete key that removes texts in a word. It deletes the text from the left of the cursor and moves the cursor to that position.
- **Caps lock key:** It is a toggle key, on pressing it every alphabetic character will be in uppercase.
- **Ctrl key:** The Ctrl key stands for the control key that is used in combination with other keys for doing a particular operation. It is the keyboard shortcut key.
- **Delete key:** It deletes or removes the characters at the current position of the cursor or also the selected object or text.
- **Enter key or Return key:** It is used to makes the computer perform an action or start a new line of writing, or it move the cursor to the beginning of the next line.
- **Esc key:** The Esc key stands for the Escape key that is used to send special codes to devices and exit from the programs and tasks and return to a previous menu.
- **Function keys:** It is a special button on a keyboard that is used for a particular operation in a program. The special keys on the computer keyboard are labeled as F1 to F12.
- **Home key:** It returns at the beginning of the line, document, page, or screen.
- **Insert key:** It toggles how text is inserted.

- **Numlock key:** It enables or disables the numeric keypad given on the right side of the computer keyboard.
- **Page up key:** It will move you up one page from the currently viewed page.
- **Page down key:** It will move you down from the currently viewed page.
- **Punctuation keys:** There are various keys on the computer keyboard that are associated with punctuation, such as Comma, Period, Semicolon, Brackets and Parenthesis.
- **Shift or Alt keys:** This key is used to move the cursor in more than one position at a time.
- **Spacebar:** This key is used for creating an empty space to separate words.
- **Tab key:** The Tab key is used to begin a line of text.
- **Numeric Keypad:** Numeric keypad is same as a simple calculator, which is present on the right-hand side of the computer keyboard.
- **Home Row Keys:** The home keys are the row of keys on the computer keyboard; your fingers rest on it when not typing. The Alphabets ASDF are home keys for left hand and LKJ along with semi-colon (;) are for the right hand. For both hands, the thumb rests on the spacebar.
- **Guide keys:** The guide keys are those keys that help in moving the cursor using the keyboard. On a computer keyboard, the F key for the left hand and J key for the right hand are guide keys. This helps touch typists in placing the fingers correctly on home keys.
- **Typing numbers:** To type numbers in a document, you have to use either the numbers keys available on the second top row of keys on the keyboard or enable Num lock of numeric keypad given on the right side.
- **Typing capital letters:** To type capital letters, you first have to click on the Caps Lock key available on the left side of the keyboard, and you will observe light on its top right side corner that shows it is on. Now whatever key you will press will come in the capital on the computer. To turn it off, again, click on the Caps lock key.
- **Typing symbols:** To type symbols given on the keyboard, you have to press the shift key along with the key with the required symbol. There are two shift keys on the keyboard; the first one is present on the left bottom side and second on the right bottom side of the keyboard. By pressing the shift key, you can access the top symbols given on keys with two characters.
- **Typing sentences:** For making sentences, you have to add space between words, to get space, press the space bar after typing one word and typing the next word.
- **Guide for typing:** For typing in a document, cursor keys are act as a guide. The cursor is a small downward indicator on the screen that flickers in a sentence while typing.
- **Creation of new lines and spaces between paragraphs:** For creating new lines and spaces between paragraphs, you have to press Enter key given on the keyboard. This moves the cursor to a new line.
- **Typing ergonomics:** Typing ergonomics is used to reduce the stress, strain, wear and tear of your joints as you repeatedly type away. This also helps in maintaining effective typewriting, along with maintaining accuracy and speed.
- **Mouse:** The mouse is a pointing device that consists of two or three buttons. One button is present on the left side, one on the right side and one in the middle.

- **Mouse Pointer:** The mouse pointer is also known as mouse arrow, mouse cursor is a graphical image that is used to control or activate certain elements in a graphical user interface.
- **Click or left click:** As mentioned above, the left click of the mouse is used to select an item. To do it, simply press the left button with your index finger.
- **Double click:** A double click on element or file will open, or it displays a dialog for editing its properties. Sometimes double click is also used to start some program or application.
- **Right-click:** The right-click anywhere in the interface will display a context sensitive menu or displays a set of commands and available options. The contents of a context menu depend on the position of the cursor when you click.
- **Scroll:** The scroll wheel or wheel mouse is a rubber or plastic wheel located between the left and right buttons. In various applications, there are scrollbars on the right side of the screen in case of having more page length than the screen or monitor length. The scroll wheel on the mouse is used to scroll the page up or down.
- **Drag and drop:** The drag and drop will select and move the item or document from one location to another without using cut and paste feature. To do it, simply take the mouse to the desired position, hold down the item by pressing the left button of the mouse, then drag the object and move the mouse to the desired location and release the left button of the mouse.
- **Rapid Typing Tutor:** Rapid Typing Tutor is free and open-source software that is designed for learning typing skills on the computer. Learning to type with a rapid typing tutor is a fun and typing game.
- **Toolbar:** Current course and current lesson control come under this section that helps the user to select the current course from the above-given list Introduction, beginner, experienced, advanced and testing modes.
- **Text Area:** Text area or text panel is an area where the user sees the text typed by them.
- **Status bar:** This bar is present on the bottom of the text area that consists of tips, progress bar, and volume control. The length of the lesson, will help a user to know about the lesson details, comes under the progress bar.
- **Virtual Keyboard:** An alternative to a physical keyboard, a virtual keyboard is a software-based keyboard used with touch screen devices. The keyboard is a digital representation of a QWERTY keyboard that appears on the screen when text input is required by the application. The user can then tap the virtual keys to type.
- **Detailed statistics:** The detailed lesson statistics display the details like typing speed, errors, and slowdown for each chapter. Mistakes done in the text can be check as they get highlighted with different colors. Where the green line indicates the good results, red color indicates bad results, and the time span exceeded by the user is indicated by yellow color. The incorrect characters and time for typing a character exceeded by users are depicted by orange color.
- **Error Window:** The detailed statistics for the current lesson can be seen on the Error tab that shows your errors and delays percentage both in the table and graphical view. This helps in understanding the hard letters to type for you.
- **Errors overview:** Errors occurred during the lesson can be checked by clicking on the Errors overview tab.

- **Editing panel:** It is the area where changes can be done in the existing course option or text of a lesson such as a navigation tree. A long text session can be split into many smaller lessons using the split lesson dialog box.
- **Table analysis text:** It displays the percentage and number of characters, words, spaces, and specific characters in the lesson.
- **CPM:** Characters per Minute are used to view the character per minute speed progress.
- **Net CPM:** Net CPM is the CPM without characters with errors.
- **KPS:** Keystroke per second.
- **CPS:** Characters per Second are used to view the character per second speed progress.
- **KPM:** Keystrokes per Minute defines the number of keystrokes in a one minute period of time.
- **Net KPM:** It is the KPM without keystrokes with errors.
- **WPS:** Words per Second, used to view the word per second speed progress.
- **WPM:** Word per Minute, used to view the word per minute speed progress.
- **Typing Rhythm:** In touch typing techniques, the typing rhythm defines that the keystrokes should come at equal intervals. In this, a slowdown indicator is used for controlling the constant speed of typing.

■ MIND MAP

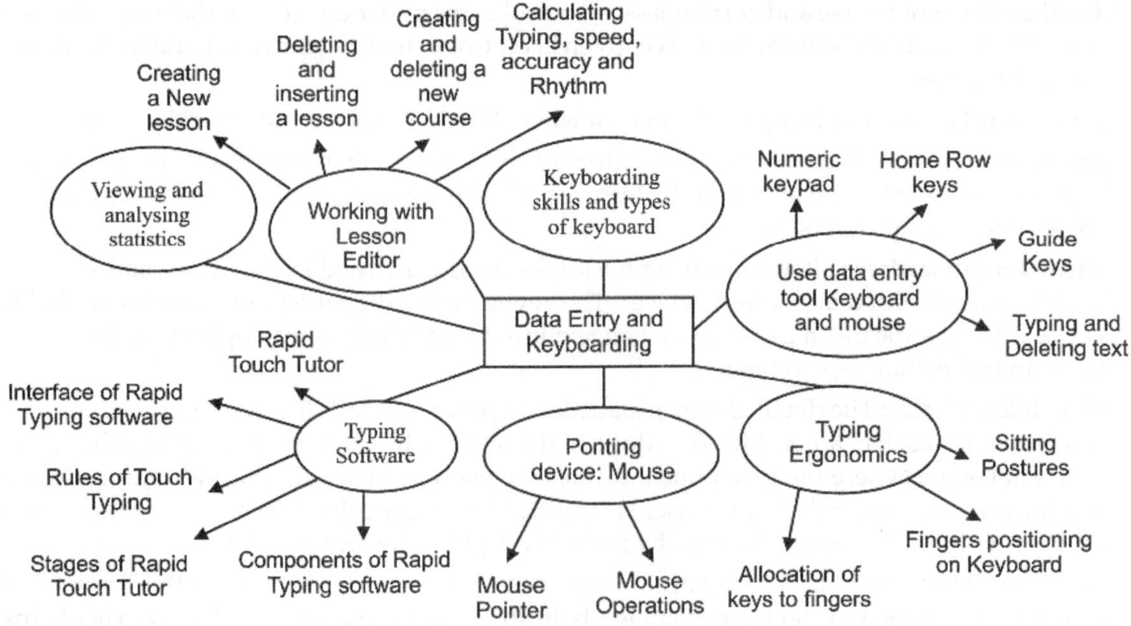

■ EXAM TIPS

1. Practice typing using Touch typing like software's that helps in increasing the speed of typing and you will also able to write about it in the exam.
2. Thoroughly check all the keys of keyboard along with its functioning.
3. In labs while working on computers follow the typing ergonomics that keep you healthy and it will also stay in your mind for long time.
4. Practice according to the allocations of fingers on the keyboard by which you will be able to learn about the allocations of keys to fingers.
5. Practically check statics and observe every color line on statistics window and also check what is indicated by it.

3

CHAPTER

Information and Communication Technology – II

■ KNOWLEDGE TIPS

- ICT stands for Information and Communication Technology that includes a set of technological resources and tools used for communication, creation, storing, managing, and disseminating information.
- UNESCO defines informatics as the science dealing with implications of realization, use, design, maintenance of information processing systems that include software, hardware, human aspects, organizational, commercial, industrial, political, and government.
- ICT is used in both personal and business life. Radio, mobile, TV, email are some of the tools of ICT. Email stands for electronic mail that reduces the load on the postal system.
- Nowadays Outlook by Microsoft, Yahoo mail, Hotmail, Rediff mail, and Gmail are major carriers of email messages.
- E-banking enables the transaction anytime, anywhere, through the Internet. Computer is one of the biggest innovations of human kind that is influencing every sphere of life.
- Combination of Hardware and Software make the computer system. Computer stands for Common oriented machines particularly used for trade and education research. Number of instructions is executed by a computer to perform a variety of tasks.
- CPU stands for Central processing unit or processors that is considered as the brain of the computer. CPU consists of ALU, MU, and CU.
- To do some specific functionality, external or internal devices can be connected to a computer system that is known as peripheral devices. The peripheral devices can be easily attached and removed from the computer system, just like a mouse, keyboard, printer, and scanners.
- Computer system consists of hardware and software; both are interdependent on each other. To start a computer, switch on the main power supply then switch on the UPS and monitor. The operating system is loaded on the RAM after completion of all the steps of BIOS, then to define user configurations, a pre-configuration start-up routine is executed by OS.
- To shut down the computer simply click on Start button present on Desktop | Click on Shut down option. In general, software is a set of instructions or programs instructing a computer to do specific tasks, or it is a generic term used to describe programs of the computer.
- System software and application software are two types of software. Operating systems, language processors, device drivers, and utility software are four categories of system software. Shell and kernel are two components of OS.
- Disk Operating System (DOS) is a type of system software that runs from a hard disk drive. Linux OS is an open and free source that was developed by Linus Torvalds in 1991 at AT & T's

Bell Laboratories. The main function of Linux OS is to manage the system resources or hardware and can act as an interface between user and computer system just like other OS.

- Edubuntu has a Graphical User Interface (GUI) that is known as Unity that allows users to interact with the computer system using graphical icons. It allows accessing your data on the web or your computer in a faster way.
- Around the world, internet is consider as a huge network of computers through which one can get any information stored in a web page on World Wide Web.
- Internet browser, Internet application software, and Web browser is important software for connecting to Internet. It is an interface between World Wide Web and user that can be GUI based like Google Chrome, Internet Explorer, Opera, Mozilla Firefox, and more, or it can text-based as Lynx.
- Webpage is a digital page that contains hyperlinks, audios, tables, text, images, and more. The Extensible Markup Language (XML), Hypertext Markup Language (HTML) and Hypertext Pre-processor (PHP), and more markup languages are used to write webpages. It is specially designed website that serves as a single point of access for information that can also be considered as personalized or categorized content library.
- Email stands for Electronic mail that is most popular internet application used to send or receive messages between various users.
- Internet helps to stay in touch with friends and your loved ones. The social media sites like Facebook, Twitter enable us to see what's happening around us in our friends' lives, and many more. Twitter is online news, and social networking service on which users post and interact with messages knows as Tweets. Facebook is the world's biggest social media website that covers around billion users worldwide. It provides user-friendly platform by creating your free account on it. YouTube is a free online video sharing service that has now acquired by Google.
- WhatsApp is a firmware and cross-platform messaging service that allows sending messages, pictures, and videos.
- 'Digital India' is a program initiated by Prime Minister Mr. Narendra Modi. The motive behind the Digital India mission is to build participative, transparent, and responsive governance to reach out the citizens.
- Aadhaar, Digilocker, Permanent Account Number (PAN), All India Council of Technical Education (AICTE), e-District, Passport, Central Board of Secondary Education (CBSE), Indian railway ticket booking, and many more are services which are provided by Digital India.

■ TECH TIPS

- **Information and communication technology (ICT):** The ICT tools are any tool that facilitates storage, dissemination, management, and creation of information and communication.
- **E-banking:** Electronic or E-banking is a product designed for the purpose of online banking that enables you to have easy and safe access to your bank account.

- **E-Governance:** The tax collection, licenses, exchange of information with citizens, and other government departments like document processing, providing government services can become possible by e-governance and digital India.
- **Email:** Email stands for electronic mail that reduces the load on the postal system. Nowadays Outlook by Microsoft, Yahoo mail, Hotmail, Rediff mail, and Gmail are the major carriers of email messages.
- **Computer:** Computer stands for Common oriented machines derived from word compute that means to calculate.
- **Hardware:** Hardware refers to the physical components of a computer. Computer Hardware is any part of the computer that we can touch these parts.
- **Software:** Software is a collection of instructions, procedures, documentation that performs different tasks on a computer system.
- **Input Unit:** Input unit is the process of entering and collecting the data into the computer. All the incoming instructions and data are converted into a pattern of binary codes, which is understood by computers.
- **Output Unit:** The processed data is displayed or print processed data in user-readable form using the output unit. There are a number of output devices attached to the computer. The output can be in the form of softcopy, hardcopy, or sound file. Some of the common output devices are monitor, printer, webcam, headphones, speaker, and many more.
- **CPU:** CPU stands for Central processing unit or processors that are considered as the brain of the computer. Processing is the action takes place to perform logical and arithmetic operations on the data to convert it into results.
- **ALU:** ALU stands for the arithmetic logic unit that is used to perform all arithmetic and logical operations on the operands. Addition, subtraction, multiplication, and division are arithmetic operations.
- **Control Unit:** The control unit controls the operation of every unit of the computer system and transfer of instructions or data in various units. Control units give a signal to components of a computer to execute any instructions.
- **Memory Unit:** It is the principle storage of computer that stores both instructions and data. These instructions and data can be stored permanently in the memory unit so that it can be retrieved when required.
- **Internal memory:** The default memory of a computer is known as internal memory, main memory, or primary memory. In primary memory, programs or instructions are stored temporarily. It is fast in speed; that's why it is known as immediate access storage but has a very little capacity of storage.
- **External memory:** It is also known as secondary or auxiliary memory and used due to expensive, temporary, and less storage capacity of internal memory. So that when required, the data can be transferred to external memory from internal memory.
- **Peripheral devices:** The input unit, output unit, and storage units are three major units of computer systems that are used for performing primary functions. To perform other functionality, one can connect some external or internal devices to computer systems that is known as peripheral devices.

- **Modem:** Modem stands for modulator/demodulator; a hardware that allows devices to connect with the Internet. It converts or modulates the analog signal from telephone cable to digital signal before transferring data to the computer system as it understands only digital signal.
- **Bluetooth adopter:** By the use of short-wavelength radio waves multiple devices can be connected through Bluetooth. It is able to connect only Bluetooth enabled devices with each other like car stereo and mobile phone, various laptops or computers, etc. The external Bluetooth can be used by embedding Bluetooth adapter in the form of a USB or small dongle.
- **Network Interface Card (NIC):** It is used to connect the computer with the local area network (LAN) and comes in the form of cards that fits in the computer motherboard expansion slot. There is a need for atleast one NIC in every computer that is a part of the network, and most of them are designed for a specific type of protocol, media, and network.
- **Wireless adaptor for Wi-Fi:** Wi-Fi stands for wireless fidelity that allows the computer to connect with the Internet or wirelessly communicate with each other. There is a need for wireless or Wi-Fi adaptor to connect wirelessly and to enable a Wi-Fi, it is plugged into peripheral component interconnect (PCI) slot present inside the computer.
- **Memory card reader:** Memory card reader enables the reading and writing to a memory card and mostly used to transfer data to a computer or other storing devices. The main function of a card is to quickly transfer files to an SD card and taking backup of the most important files.
- **Smartphones:** Smartphone is a multipurpose computing device that can connect the computer to the internet through Hotspot feature and also enable the exchange of information with the computer.
- **Digital camera:** It is a hardware device used to capture recording, still pictures, storing videos with sound in the digital formats. The digital or 0's and 1's format is the only format which computer understands, and these are tiny dots pixels stored in digital cameras.
- **Software System:** It is collections of single or multiple programs that manage or control the overall performance and operation of a computer system. It is an interface between computer and user that is used for reading data from input devices, transmissions of information from input to output devices, and it also checks the order of working internal and external peripheral devices.
- **Operating System:** It is an interface between hardware and software of a computer that manages the overall functionality of the computer and its resources. It also monitors and controls the execution of other applications and programs by performing sending output to monitor, recognizing input from the keyboard, and controlling peripheral devices.
- **Shell:** It is an interface and outermost layer of OS that handle the interaction with users.
- **Kernel:** It is an interface and core component of OS that handles the interaction between data processing and applications done at the hardware level.
- **Batch OS:** The batch OS users cannot directly interacts with the computer. In this type of OS, every user prepares their own job on a punch card like an offline device and submits it to the computer operator.
- **Time-sharing or multi-tasking OS:** The Multi-tasking OS enables users located at different shell or terminal to use a single computer system at the same time. The OS that is able to perform multiple tasks or processes using a single CPU or processor, then it is known as Multi-tasking OS.
- **Real-Time OS (RTOS):** RTOS is designed to handle real-life scenarios problems and has very short respond time to inputs; it can prioritize the processes and able to work independently. It is used in space software systems, military software systems, and booking air tickets.

- **Single user OS:** In this type of OS, only single user can access the resources at a particular time. Microsoft Windows 3.1, Microsoft DOS, and Microsoft 95 are some of the common single-user OS.
- **Multi-user OS:** It allows us to use more than one user to use the same computer at the same time. Unix, Linux, Microsoft window 2000, and many more are some of the multi-user OS. Windows 2000 was the first version of windows that allow creating multiple user accounts on a single machine.
- **Distributed OS:** It runs on computers located at different geographical areas interconnected through networks. It uses processors located in different machines to provide a very fast computation to the users. The linked machines are allowed to access software, data, and process the tasks over a geographical network.
- **Multi-threading OS:** This type of OS allows us to run different parts of the program and application simultaneously. The execution response of some processes can get delayed due to the feature of multithreading. Disk Operating System (DOS) is a type of system software that runs from a hard disk drive. This also refers to the specific family of DOS, which is known as a Microsoft disk operating system (MS-DOS).
- **Linux:** Linux OS is an open and free source that was developed by Linus Torvalds in 1991 at AT & T's Bell Laboratories. The main function of Linux OS is to manage the system resources or hardware and can act as an interface between user and computer system just like other OS. It was designed by considering UNIX compatibility; that's why its functioning is similar to UNIX.
- **EDUBUNTU:** It has a Graphical User Interface (GUI) that is known as Unity that allows users to interact with the computer system using graphical icons. It allows accessing your data on the web or your computer in a faster way.
- **Desktop:** Desktop is the first thing that appears on turning on the computer. It has two bars, one on the left and the other on top. A desktop wallpaper is the image at the background of a desktop. Icons are small labeled symbols and pictures present on the desktop that are used to open some documents or programs.
- **Internet:** Internet is considered as a huge network of computers through which one can get any information stored on a web page on the World Wide Web. It is one of the largest databases available to us permanently and has become an important part of life.
- **Internet browser:** Internet browser, Internet application software, and Web browser is an important software for connecting to the Internet. It is an interface between the World Wide Web and user that can be GUI based.
- **Web portal:** It is a specially designed website that serves as a single point of access for information that can also be considered as a personalized or categorized content library. It helps in search navigation, information integration, notification, and personalization.
- **Email account:** Email account is an electronic mailbox on a network where a user sends emails or messages. As mentioned above user must have a register email address to send messages, and the user uses these account name and password to send messages and mention the email address of the user to who he/she wants to send a mail.
- **Email address:** The email address of the user is a must to use the services the email services that are a unique name to identify accounts on a network. There is a need for email address of both the sender and receiver to send and receive emails.

- **Twitter:** Twitter is an online news and social networking service on which users post and interacts with messages known as tweets.
- **Facebook:** Facebook is the world's biggest social media website that covers around billion users worldwide. It provides user-friendly platform by creating your free account on it. When it comes in existence, it can only be used in PC, but now it becomes a default app in almost every mobile phone and tablet.
- **Youtube:** It is a free online video sharing service that has now acquired by Google. One can search for video, songs, movies, exercise tips, comedy, and tutorial to learn something on it. Any person can upload their video on YouTube by creating user Id and password, and all other person can see it.
- **WhatsApp:** It is a firmware and cross-platform messaging service that allows sending messages, pictures, and videos. One can also do voice or video call with other person across the world.
- **Digital India:** 'Digital India' is a program initiated by Prime Minister Mr. Narendra Modi. The motive behind the Digital India mission is to build participative, transparent, and responsive governance to reach out the citizens. It aims to provide all services electronically and promote digital literacy in India with the help of digital technologies, which includes the concept of cloud computing, and mobile applications have emerged as the catalysts for express economic growth and citizen empowerment.

■ MIND MAP

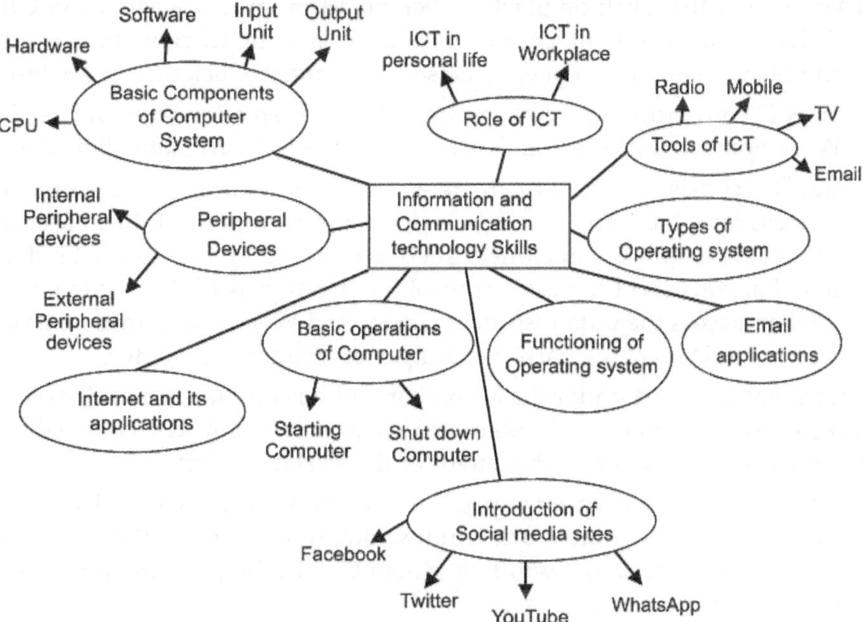

■ EXAM TIPS

1. Observe the usage of ICT in various workplaces.
2. Observe your computer system and check each and every component and name it
3. Practically turn ON or OFF the computer step by step that helps you in remembering the steps for long life.
4. Check for different types of operating systems then observe the changes in each individual.

DIGITAL DOCUMENTATION

■ KNOWLEDGE TIPS

- Word processor allows user to organize and present text on a page or several pages. The text organized in this way is referred to as a document.
- Formatting, graphic, ease and speed, printing, storage, mail merge, vocabulary and spell check are the basic features of Microsoft word 2010. Notepad and WordPad are the desktop based applications.
- To open MS word 2010, Click on Start > Click on all programs > Microsoft Office > Microsoft Word 2010. To save a Document, click on File tab > Save. By Clicking on Save As, you can save your existing file with another name. To close a Document, Click on File > Close.
- Various parts of Word processor Window are Title Bar, Menu Bar, Standard Tool Bar, Formatting Tool Bar, Work Space, Vertical Scroll Bar, Horizontal Scroll Bar, Status Bar, Zoom Control.
- File in Menu Bar consist of items to create a new document, save a document, access remote servers, to access templates and wizards and print a document. Edit in Menu Bar consists of items or commands to edit the document such as copy, cut, paste, undo, Find and Replace, etc. View in Menu Bar consists of items for controlling the display of the document, such as Open or close the sidebar, access the data resources, Zoom and Web layout. Insert in Menu Bar consists of commands to insert images, charts and shapes or Header and Footer.
- The standard toolbar is just under the Menu bar and it is also known as docked or fixed toolbar. The floating toolbar is just below the Standard Toolbar. It is context sensitive that shows the tools relevant to the current position of the cursor or the selected object.
- The Status Bar displays the number of pages, word count, language used and zooming function, etc. Scroll Bar helps to move the work window down or up and left or right by which we can check the non-visible part on the window. Zoom Control help in changing the scale of the text and pictures in the document for view.
- The mouse pointer is also known mouse arrow, mouse cursor is a graphical image that is used to control or activate certain elements in a graphical user interface.
- To open an existing document, Click on File tab > Open or Click on Quick access toolbar > Open

- To perform Undo action, click on Undo button given in Quick Access Bar. To perform Redo action, click on Redo button given in Quick Access Bar. To save changes done in the document, click on the file tab > Save
- If we want to create or use the same data, then copy command of MS Word 2010 can be used. To copy a data, Select the text > Right click on it > Select copy command. Shortcut key to copy the text is Ctrl + C. The work of paste command is to place the copied text in the desired location. After copying a data to paste it, Right click on desired location > Select paste command. Shortcut key to paste a copy is Ctrl + V.
- The cut command will remove that data from the particular location and now the text can be pasted in another location.
- To select a non-consecutive text item using mouse, select the starting text then hold down the mouse to select next piece of text. To select a vertical block of text item using mouse, Select the vertical block or column by mouse by simply taking mouse to starting point and then taking it towards rest of the block that you want to select.
- Find command in word will find the particular text for user. Find command is available in Editing group of Home tab.
- To find a text or word, click on drop down button "Find" given in the editing group of home tab > Select find > type the word in dialog box open in left side of document.
- Shortcut key to open a navigation bar is Ctrl + F.
- In word, we can also replace the particular word with another word. To replace the text, Click on Replace command given in Editing group of Home tab > A new dialog box will come > Write the word which you want to replace in "Find What" column > Write the new word you want to add > Click on either Replace or Replace All.
- Shortcut to open Go to Page dialog box: Press Ctrl + G.
- Non-printing characters are such paragraph marks, line breaks, tab stops, spaces, etc. that do not appear on the screen.
- In MS word 2010 there is built-in feature of checking and correcting the errors. The red wavy line highlights the errors related to spelling mistakes. To remove these errors, Right click on text that have red wavy line > Select the match word. The green line under the text shows the grammatical mistake. Blue wavy line will come under the word or sentence if a correct work is used in wrong place.
- The synonyms, antonyms, word substitute, and alternative spelling comes in word through thesaurus. F7 key is a shortcut to use Spelling and Grammar tool. Shift + F7 is a shortcut key to open Thesaurus in the document.
- There are various types of fonts available in MS Word 2010 along with various sizes. Font type and font size can be changed through Font group of Home tab.
- To perform changes in font type, click on home tab > click on font type drop down arrow > select the font type. To perform changes in font size, click on home tab > click on font size drop down arrow > select the font size. In Home tab various font effects are available that can be used to highlight the text or making your document more attractive.

- To change the case of text, Click on Change case > Select the required type from drop down bar. Subscript write the text below the baseline and superscript write the text above the baseline.
- By default, text is align towards left side. In left alignment there is little space in the right side. Center alignment will align the text in the center of the document and leave little space from both the ends. In right alignment the text is align towards right side and leave little space in the left. In Justify alignment text is evenly aligned between the left and right side. To perform vertical text alignment, Click on the Page Layout tab > Page setup dialog box > Layout tabs.
- Indent is the distance of page margins and text boundaries. To perform Indent by using buttons. Select the text > Click on Decrease or Increase Indent. We can indent the text using indent marker given on the ruler.
- There are two types of list name as Ordered and Unordered. Bullets is used to create an unordered list. To create a list by using bullet, create a list > select it > click on the drop-down button on Bullets command from paragraph group > select the style. Numbering is used to create an ordered list. To create a list using numbering, create a list > select it > click on the drop-down button on Numbering command from paragraph group > select the style.
- We can also create our own style of numbering and bullet by defining a new bullet and new numbering style given in drop-down of both bullet and numbering command.
- Tables is a combination of row and column where texts are arranged. The cell is the combination of row and column. Tables can be created by two methods: Grid and dialog box.
- To create a table using grid, Click on Insert Tab > Table command Drop down arrow > Drag the mouse pointer over the grid on number of rows and columns required by you. To create a table by using Dialog box, Click on the Insert Tab > Select the table drop down arrow > Select Insert Table option. User can also create their own table by using Draw table option given in the table drop down arrow.
- Tab key can be used to move from one row or column to another. Using Formatting the complete appearance of table can be changed according to our requirement that comes as more attractive and presentative style of table. Two label of Table tools are Design and Layout.
- The overall appearance of the table can be change by using design label given in the Table tools. There are inbuilt styles of tables in word that contains option of changing the color, appearance and borders of a table. When you click on Layout label various groups of changing the table style will come in the ribbon bar.
- Text can be converted into Table by using Convert Text to Table command in Table drop down. The text must be either separated by commas or tabs. The table can be converted into a text using Convert Table to Text command of Data group in Layout label. The text converted from table can be separated by Tabs, Paragraph marks and commas.
- To add border to a page, open a document > Write a text > Click on the page Layout tab >select Page Borders from Page Background group > Border and shading dialog box will appear > Select box option or style of border as per your requirements.
- To apply shading on the page, Select the text of a page > Click on Page Layout > Page and Border command from Page Background group > Shading tab > Do needful changes in Fill and Patterns section.

- To apply border to a Paragraph or text, open a document > Write a text > Select the paragraph or text > Select drop down arrow of Bottom Borders command from Paragraph Group > Select Border and Shading option > a dialog box will appear.
- To add border to a paragraph or text, open a document > Write a text > Select the paragraph or text > Select drop down arrow of Bottom Borders command from Paragraph Group > Select Border and Shading option > a dialog box will appear.
- To print a document in desired manner a page orientation and margins are used. Around the edges of a document there is blank space that is known as margins.
- To set page margin by using Page setup dialog box, Open the document > click on Page Layout tab > Margin drop down arrow > Select the required margin option.
- Portrait is a default orientation of Word. The page is taller than wider in case of Portrait orientation on other hand page become more wider and less taller in case of landscape orientation.
- To apply page orientation, open a document > click on Page Layout tab > Drop down arrow of orientation > Select orientation of your style. Ctrl + M is the shortcut key to indent a paragraph from left side.
- Through Mail Merge feature a piece of text can be sent to multiple addresses. With the feature of mail merge we can merge the main document that can be certificates or letter with mailing address of various persons.
- In MS Word, Corresponding values are kept in data source that is a set of mailing address in multiple rows and columns that is also known as database.

■ TECH TIPS

- **Word Processor:** Word processor allow user to organize and present text on a page or several pages. The text organized in this way is referred to as a document.
- **Notepad:** Notepad is a generic text editor included with all versions of the file containing special formatting or is not a plaintext file, it cannot be read in Microsoft Notepad. The image is a small example of what the Microsoft Notepad may look like while running.
- **WordPad:** WordPad is a basic word processor available in every version of Microsoft's operating systems since Windows 95. It can be used to create and modify documents. Although slower to load than Notepad, it can handle graphics and rich formatting, unlike notepad, along with handling larger files. WordPad is well preferred for taking quick notes and text-based writing.
- **Title Bar:** It is present on the top and middle of word window. Both the name of program and its currently used document is display on it.
- **Quick access toolbar:** It is located on the top left side of the title bar. The frequently used common buttons are present on it. Redo, Undo, and Save are the three buttons that are present by default on it. We can remove or add another button through the drop-down arrow present on it.
- **Window control buttons:** The window control buttons consist of three buttons named as minimize, restore or maximize and close button. Each have their own functioning as to reduce the size of the word window a minimize button is clicked.

- **File Tab:** In word 2010 there is file tab in the place of office button in word 2007. By clicking on it you will get various options like opening a File, New, Save, Save as, Print, etc.
- **Ribbon:** On clicking on any tab a ribbon appears. It contains tab, groups, and commands. On top of ribbon button there are eight tabs present which contains groups of related commands organized in groups.
- **Menu Bar:** Menu bar is located below the Title bar. On selecting any menus from menu bar, a submenu drops down to show further options or commands.
- **Rulers:** There are two types of ruler bars name as vertical and horizontal bars. The horizontal bar is present on the top that is used to set tab stops and margins on other hand the vertical alignment of text is formatted by using vertical ruler bar present on the left side of the Word Window.
- **Document or work area:** This is the blank area where user type, edit, and format the text. User start writing from vertical line called insertion point or cursor.
- **Tool Bar:** The toolbar, also called bar or standard toolbar, is a row of boxes, present at the top of an application window, that control various functions of the software. Tool bar appears below the Menu bar. In MS Word there are two types of Tool bar, Standards toolbar and Floating toolbar.
- **Standard Toolbar:** The standard toolbar is just under the Menu bar and it is also known as docked or fixed toolbar. It consists of command in the form of icons and is consistent across the MS Word applications.
- **Floating Toolbar:** The floating toolbar is present just below the Standard Toolbar. It is context sensitive that shows the tools relevant to the current position of the cursor or the selected object.
- **Status Bar:** The status bar is on the left bottom of the Window that displays the number of pages, word count, language used and zooming function, etc.
- **Scroll Bar:** It helps to move the work window down or up and left or right by which we can check the non-visible part on the Window. There are two types of scrollbars name as horizontal and vertical.
- **Zoom Control:** It help in changing the scale of the text and pictures in the document for view. It does not affect the physical document.
- **Workspace:** It is the area reserved for typing and adding pictures or clipart.
- **Mouse:** Mouse, sometimes called a pointer, is a hand-operated input device used to manipulate objects on a computer screen.
- **Mouse pointer:** The mouse pointer is also known mouse arrow, mouse cursor that is a graphical image that is used to control or activate certain elements in a graphical user interface.
- **Undo:** Undo is a function performed to reverse the action of an earlier action. For example, the undo function can undo deleted text in a word processor. Some software programs may also have the capability of performing multiple undo's.
- **Redo:** Redo means re-doing the last action undone. For example, after undoing the bold command, if you redo the action, the text will again become bold.

- **Copy the Data:** If you want to create or use the same data, then copy command of MS Word can be used. Either single or multiple copies of data can be created by using single command without affecting the existing data. This will save time and efforts that user has to put in writing the same data again in different location.
- **Paste the Data:** The copied data will be pasted in location where we want to use it. The work of the paste command is to place the copied text in the desired location.
- **Cut the Data:** In case of copy command, we will get the copy of that data which is further being pasted on different locations. On the other hand, the cut command will remove that data from the particular location, and it will paste the text in another location.
- **Selecting Text:** To perform the operation of copy and paste or cut and paste operation, you have to select the text that will be highlighted after selection. Firstly text is selected before editing the text. As you can do editing part of selected text.
- **Selecting Non-consecutive text items:** Sometimes there can be cases in which you have to select a part of the text from a paragraph instead of continuous text. In Word processor you can either use keyboard or mouse to select the non-consecutive text.
- **Non-printing characters:** Non-printing characters are paragraph marks, line breaks, tab stops, spaces, etc. that do not appear on the screen. Other characters that are visible on the screen are alphabet, numbers, punctuation marks, etc.
- **Grammatical mistake:** The green line under the text shows the grammatical mistake. In those cases, simply right click on the text and you will get suggestions for writing the correct word. Another option is to select the Grammar icon on dialog box, which appears once you click on the text having green line.
- **Spelling mistake:** The red wavy line highlights the errors related to spelling mistakes.
- **Contextual mistake:** The blue line will come under the word or sentence if a correct word is used in wrong place. Or if the sentence making is not right. These types of errors can be removed by right clicking on it and selecting the right option.
- **Change case:** Using this command user can change the selected text into Sentence case, lowercase, UPPERCASE, Capitalize each word and Toggle case.
- **Text Alignment:** The position of text between the page margins is known as text alignment. Horizontal and vertical are the two types of text alignment present in word.
- **Horizontal Text Alignment:** By default, the text is aligned on the left side of the document and the right margins in the document is known as horizontal text alignment. There are mainly four text alignment styles comes under this category.
- **Indent:** Indent is the distance of page margins and text boundaries. Tab key are mostly used to indent the text and it is mainly use in indenting a single line of text rather than for multiple lines or paragraphs. To perform this simply take mouse in front of first line of text and press Tab key.
- **Bullets:** Mainly unordered list are created by using bullet as there is no sequence of items in it. There are various styles of bullets available in Word.
- **Numbering:** Ordered list are created by using number as there is sequence of items in it. There are various styles of numbering available in Word.

- **Table:** A table is an arrangement of information in cells that make comparing and contrasting information easier.
- **Page Margins:** Around the edges of a document there is blank space known as margins. The header, footer, and page number or extra information like items can be written in the margins.
- **Page Orientation:** By default, there is Portrait orientation of page in word 2010 but you can switch to Landscape orientation when require. The page is taller than wider in case of Portrait orientation on other hand, page become more wider and less taller in case of landscape orientation.
- **Mail Merge:** Mail merge is a feature within most data processing applications that enables users to send a similar letter or document to multiple recipients. It enables connecting a single form template with a data source that contains information about the recipient's name, address and other predefined and supported data.

■ MIND MAP

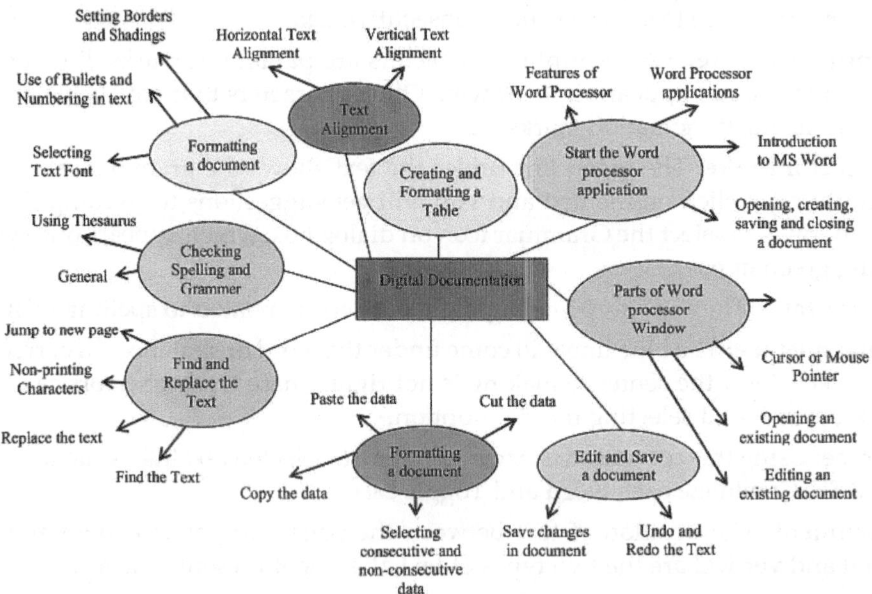

■ EXAM TIPS

1. Do all the things practically on computer to know exactly about various parts of Word Processor.
2. Send invitation to 2-3 Ids using mail merge in one go to keep the steps of it in mind for long time.
3. Make a document and apply all the formatting functions on it such as adding border, inserting image, adding color, etc.
4. Make list in a table then add more row and column. After that try splitting and merging function.

4 CHAPTER Entrepreneur Skills – II

■ KNOWLEDGE TIPS

- Business is an economic activity that is related to regular and continuous production and distribution of services or goods that satisfy human needs. All business activities are classified into four broad categories: Service, Manufacturing, Merchandising, and Hybrid.
- An entrepreneur can be an educator, businessman, artist, restaurateur, inventor, or professional.
- Business enterprises may be organized in various forms including Joint Stock Company, cooperative society, sole proprietorship, and partnership firm.
- Joint stock company forms a business organization as a voluntary association of persons to carry on business. Cooperative society is a society whose purpose is to render services to its members and to the public. In Sole proprietorship, business is owned by a single person who provides the entire capital, bears all the risks, and independently manages it. Partnership is another form of non-cooperative form of enterprise.
- In this more than one person carry a lawful business and share its profits. The word Entrepreneur is derived from the French verb enterprendre that means to undertake and it is used to define a person who undertakes risk to start their own business.
- An Entrepreneur is a designer or creator who designs new businesses and ideas according to their own passion and requirements of market. Entrepreneurship development is the process of improvement the skills and knowledge of entrepreneurs through various training and classroom programs.
- Pre-training and initial phase, training or development phase and post training or follow up phase are three phases of entrepreneurship development. Economic, social, and psychological factors are affecting the growth of entrepreneurship.
- Characteristics of entrepreneurship are systematic activity, powerful and lawful activity, creative activity, risk bearing activity, gap filling, initiative taking, and innovation.
- Role of entrepreneurship are classified into three categories: economic development, social development, and psychological development. Rewards of entrepreneurship are: be the boss, freedom to does anything, building an enterprise, own schedule, business from home, and excitement.

■ TECH TIPS

- **Entrepreneur:** Entrepreneur is a self-employed person who is willing to take a risk and start a business with a new idea. All self-employed persons, like shopkeepers, are not entrepreneurs until a new idea or method is not introduced by them in business.

- **Business:** Business is an economic activity that is related to regular and continuous production and distribution of services or goods that satisfy human needs. Businesses can be for non-profit or for profit organizations that cater to the society needs.
- **Service:** It is a business that provides products with no physical form. These companies or firms provide expertise, professional skills, advice and other similar services.
- **Manufacturing:** It is concerned with the transformation and manufacturing of raw materials, labor, and other production processes to manufacture goods. To make new products raw materials are bought by manufacturers.
- **Merchandising:** It is also known as trading or buy and sell business. In this, merchandise business firms buy products at wholesale prices and further sell it at retail prices to other customers or retailers.
- **Joint stock company:** It forms a business organization as a voluntary association of persons to carryon business. It normally gives legal status and is subjected to certain legal regulations or association of persons who are contributing money for a common purpose.
- **Cooperative society:** It is a society whose purpose is to render services to its members and to the public. It is democratically operated and controlled on a non-profit basis as their basic motive is to meet social, economic and cultural needs of its member.
- **Sole proprietorship:** This business is owned by a single person who provides the entire capital, bears all the risks and independently manages it. This form is mainly adopted for small scale independent businesses, thus it is also known as one man business organization.
- **Partnership:** It is another form of non-cooperative form of enterprise. In this more than one person carry a lawful business and share its profits. Even losses are borne equally by themselves.
- **Entrepreneurship:** Entrepreneurship is the art of starting a new company or business that makes creative products, process, and services.

■ MIND MAP

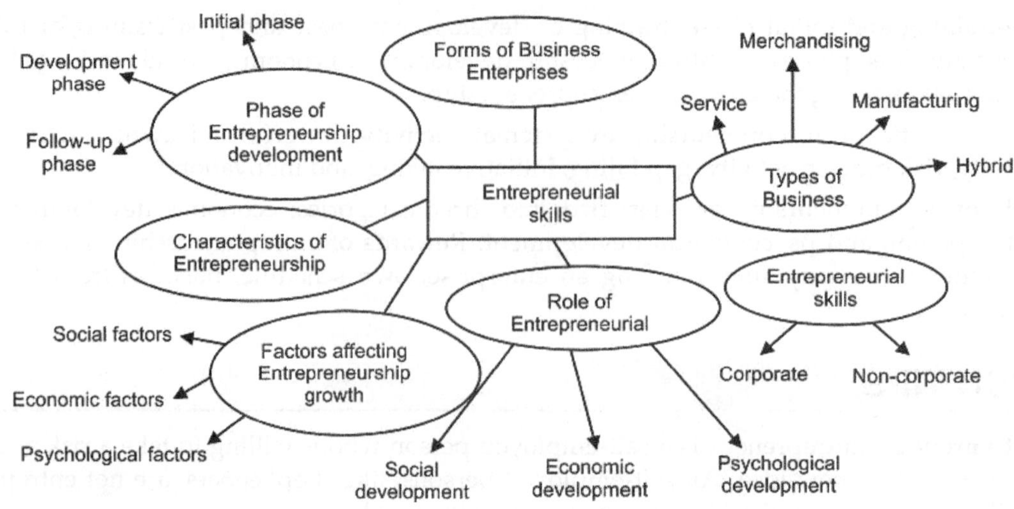

■ EXAM TIPS

1. Read the Stories of great entrepreneurs to know more about entrepreneurs and important skills required to be a successful entrepreneurs.
2. Make a list of various shops, factories in your city then divide it into different category of business activities.
3. Make a presentation on various forms of Business Enterprises and student will cover the detail that helps in easy learning of all types.
4. Search and write the advantages of being working in partnership.

ELECTRONIC SPREADSHEET

■ KNOWLEDGE TIPS

- Workbook is the another name of MS excel file used by users to write and store their data. To launch the spreadsheet program, Click on Start > Click on all programs > Microsoft Office > Microsoft Excel 2010
- On top and middle of excel window there is title bar. Quick access toolbar is located in the top left side of title bar.
- There are eight Tabs in MS excel. Ribbon appears on clicking of any tab and it contains various tabs, groups and commands.
- Worksheet is a grid consists of rows and columns in which data is enter. Cell is a intersection of rows and column. Rows are horizontal arrangement of Cells. Column is the vertical arrangement of cells. Limits of row are 1048576. Maximum number of columns in Excel are 16384
- Scrollbar helps to move page down or up and left or right the work window. Data can be directly enter in Active cell. Formulae can directly enter in Formulae bar. Extension of MS excel file is .xlsx.
- To create a new workbook, Click on File tab > New > Blank Workbook > Create. Ctrl + N is the shortcut key to create new workbook. By default sheet1 is the active worksheet.
- To insert a worksheet, Right click on Sheet3 > select Insert option > Worksheet > OK or click on Insert worksheet button present next to Sheet3 tab or Press Shift + F11.
- To save a workbook or worksheet, Click on File > Save > Select the location from given list in the left of Save As dialog box > Enter name in file name text box.
- To rename a worksheet, Double click on the sheet tab given in bottom left side > Type a name > Press Enter button given on keyboard or Right click on sheet tab > select rename option > Assign new name by typing on it.
- To delete a worksheet, Right click on desired worksheet > Select Delete option.

- To move a worksheet, Right click on desired sheet tab > Select Move or Copy option. To move worksheet between two workbook, Click on To book drop down list > Choose new book option > Click on OK.
- To open existing workbook or Worksheet, Click on File > Open or Click on Open button from drop down arrow of Customize quick access Toolbar Or press CTRL + O key.
- To close a workbook, Click on File Tab > Close Or Press both Ctrl + W. In MS Excel Spreadsheet, there is need to select the cell before entering data in worksheet or cell.
- To select a cell simply position the pointer in that particular cell. You can enter label, values or formula data in the cell. Label is any text that can be letters, numbers and special symbols that entered using keyboard. By default labels are aligned in left side.
- Value is the numeric data consists of only numbers. By defaults they are aligned on right side. Various forms of values are integer, decimal, etc. Formula is the expression that begins with an equals "=" sign. Formula is always start by "=" and followed by values, cell address and functions.
- In MS Excel Spreadsheet or spreadsheet you can also enter formulae with cell addresses and operators as like values and operators. The "+" sign is used to perform the addition on data given in the MS Excel Spreadsheet. The "-" sign is used to perform the subtraction on data given in the MS Excel Spreadsheet. The "*" sign is used to perform the multiplication on data given in the MS Excel Spreadsheet. The "/" sign is used to perform the division on data given in the MS Excel Spreadsheet.
- In MS Excel Spreadsheet there are predefined formulas or functions that can be used to perform the required calculations. Such as SUM(), AVERAGE(), MAX(), MIN(), COUNT, TODAY().
- To change the format of number, Select the Cells > Click on Format button drop down arrow given in the Cells group of Home tab.
- There are various options to format the text like text alignment, color, style, size, font, Wrap text, etc.
- Various formatting options available on the formatting toolbar are the font, font size, bold, italic, underline, left alignment, center alignment, right alignment, increase decimal places, and decrease decimal places.
- To open the Format dialog box, select the cells, and click on the Format command in Cells group of Home tab drop-down menu. Select the cell, and Format Cells dialog box will open. The shortcut key to open Format cells dialog box: press Ctrl +O.
- There are some cases in which there is a need to format the number to a fixed number of decimal places. These cases can come when the division of different numbers results in varied decimal places in the quotient.
- There are some cases in which there is a need to format a range of cells to be seen as labels. These cases can come in telephone numbers in which every country STD code starts with 0.
- There are some cases in which there is a need to format a range of cells as scientific. These cases can come into entering the date.

- There are some cases in which there is a need to format a range of cells to display time. These cases can come in the time indicated on a computer.
- There are some cases in which there is a need to format the alignment of a cell range. These cases can come when we enter values and labels as by default, and labels are aligned to the left side, and values are aligned by the right side.
- To speed up the work, you can use a mouse to drag and drop the contents of one cell to another cell in the spreadsheet. In MS Excel spreadsheet, there are some other tools that help in automating the input, mainly in case of repetitive tasks.
- In the MS Excel spreadsheet Fill Handle tool, you can fill the next cells by dragging it with the next predefined value. For example, you want to fill the roll numbers, month, week, days, then you can input one or two in sequence, then select them and drag it to the next cell.
- Fill handle of a cell is the small black square in the bottom of the right corner of the last selected cell.
- In Excel there is feature of referencing which is the way to refer any formula or function of one cell to the next cell along the row or column. By default all the cell references are relative references in which the formula gets copied in the new cell when you select any formula and drag it to new cell.
- There are cases when you don't want a cell reference to change when copied to other cells as happen in relative referencing. In those cases absolute referencing is used as it will not change when copied and filled in another cell.
- To use Absolute referencing a $ symbol is used before the column name and row number that make it constant for any formula.
- It is the combination of relative and absolute referencing. It is used when we have to make some row number and column name constant and some has to vary accordingly.
- In case of representation of large amount of data a visual representation is always preferred. That is the reason there is Charts feature in every spreadsheet so that data can be visually represented in different ways.
- A chart is a graphical representation of data in which the data is represented by symbols like bars in a bar chart, lines in a line chart and slices in a pie chart. Column charts are used for comparing several items in a specific range of values. Line chart is one of the most frequently used chart types that is used to show trends over a period of time. Pie chart represents the distribution or proportion of each data item over a total value. Bar charts are used for comparing several categories of data. Area charts are ideal for clearly illustrating the magnitude of change between two or more data points. Scatter charts are also known as XY scatter plot charts that are very good for showing the correlations between two sets of values. Bubble chart is like a scatter chart with an additional third column that specify the size of the bubbles.
- To create a chart in spreadsheet, Select the range of data > Click on Insert menu bar > Click on Chart and Chart Wizard dialog box will open > Choose the required type of chart > Click on Finish button.

■ TECH TIPS

- **Spreadsheet:** A spreadsheet or worksheet is a file made of numerical data. What makes a spreadsheet software program unique is its ability to calculate values using mathematical cells.
- **Title Bar:** On top and middle of excel window there is title bar. Both the name of program and its currently used document name is display on it. It also contains minimize, maximize and Close buttons.
- **Quick access toolbar:** It is located in the top left side of title bar. The frequently used common buttons are present on it. Redo, Undo and save are three buttons that are present by default on it. We can remove or add other button through the drop down arrow present on it
- **Tabs:** Below the title bar there is tabs that contains various group of command used to work in word. Some of the tabs in excel are home, insert, page layout, formulas, data, review, view.
- **Ribbon:** On clicking of any tab a ribbon appears. It contains tab, groups and commands. On top of ribbon button there are 7 tabs that contains groups of related commands. All related commands are organized in groups.
- **Name Box:** Active cell name is present in Name box that is located on left side before the Formula box in top of worksheet.
- **Formula Bar:** In formula bar user can directly enter the formulae or data or click on cell that contains formula then it will start appearing on formula bar. It is located in right side of Name box.
- **Scrollbar:** It helps in page down or up and left or right the work window by which we can check the non-visible part on the window. There are two types of scrollbars name as horizontal and vertical. The horizontal bar helps in navigating from left to right and it is present in bottom above the status bar. Other type is vertical bar that is present in right and used to navigate the document from top to bottom.
- **Status Bar:** Below the horizontal scrollbar there is status bar that gives working worksheet status like sheet number, active working mode, zoom functioning along with other spreadsheet related important information.
- **Sheet Tabs:** The sheet tabs are available on left bottom side of excel file. By defaults there are three sheets name as Sheet1, Sheet2 and Sheet3. The particular worksheet become active by clicking on it from bottom sheet tabs. More sheets can be added in it by clicking on inserting worksheet given next to Sheet3. The name of these sheets can be changed by right click on particular sheet and selecting rename option or by double clicking on name and entering the required name in it.
- **Quick access toolbar:** It is located on the top left side of the title bar. The frequently used common buttons are present on it. We can remove or add another button through the drop-down arrow present on it.
- **Toolbars:** The toolbar, also called bar or standard toolbar, is a row of boxes, often at the top of an application window, that control various functions of the software. The boxes often contain images that correspond with the function they control.
- **Standard toolbar:** It shows the icons for most common operations such as editing, arranging, filtering, and more.
- **Formatting toolbar:** It consists of most common operations related to datasheet formatting such as font selection, size of text, alignment, cell value formatting and indentation, and more.

- **Control buttons:** On the top right side of the Title bar, there are control buttons such as minimize, maximize, and close.
- **Column and row heading:** The column and row heading are the names of rows and columns.
- **Active cell:** A thick black color boundary appears on the cell when we click on it that makes it different from non-active cells. Users can enter or edit data only in active cells. The name given to this highlighted box is the cell pointer.
- **Worksheet:** Worksheet is a grid that consists of number of rows and columns in which data is enter by user. By default there are three worksheet in Excel, name as Sheet 1, Sheet2 and Sheet3 displayed at bottom left side.
- **Cell:** Cell is a intersection of row and column. Number of cells makes a worksheet. Each row is identified by row number and column number that is known as address of cell. For e.g., A1, B2, N6, etc. User can enter data, text, formulas and number in each cell and upto 32767 characters can be come single cells.
- **Row:** In excel rows are horizontal arrangement of cells and it is numbered in numerical digit start from 1, 2, 3, 4, 5 and so on.
- **Column:** In excel columns are align vertically and alphabets are assigned to it start from A, B, C, so on.
- **Row header:** On left hand side of sheet there is numeric number starts from 1 known as row header. It ranges from 1 to 1048576.
- **Column header:** On top border of sheet there is alphabets starts from A and go first go from A to Z, AA…AZ, BA, BB, BC…..BZ, CA,. There are 16384 columns in every worksheet in Excel.
- **Column Range:** Number of cells selected or spread across the column. In this case the cell address is represented by single column letter and multiple row number in a sequence.
- **Row Range:** Number of cells selected or spread across the row. In this case the row address is represented by single row number and multiple columns in a sequence.
- **Label:** Text that can be letters, numbers and special symbols that entered using keyboard. By default labels are aligned in left side.
- **Values:** Numeric data consists of only numbers. By defaults they are aligned on right side. Various forms of values are integer, decimal, etc.
- **Formulae:** Expression that begins with an equals "=" sign. Formula always start by "=" and followed by values, cell address and functions. After entering the formula in a cell, then the value of the equation is displayed in the cell and formulas bar contains the formula.
- **SUM( ):** Just like + sign in basic formulas a SUM() function will add all the numbers given in the arguments between the parenthesis of sum function. For example: SUM(B2:B6)
- **AVERAGE( ):** The arithmetic mean and average of the arguments is return by AVERAGE function. In arguments user can enter the range of cells, direct numbers, both numbers and cell reference. For example: AVERAGE(B2:B6)
- **MAX( ):** The MAX function will return the largest value from specified arguments in parenthesis of MAX function. It accept only numeric data and logical values as arguments and return zero 0 in other cases. Syntax: MAX(starting range: Ending range)

- **TODAY( ):** The current date of particular cell can be display using the function TODAY( ). Example type =TODAY() function in cell E3 it will display the date of E3 cell.
- **Formatting tool:** To make the worksheet looks presentable and make it attractive for reader MS Excel spreadsheet, formatting features can be used that improves the overall look of the spreadsheet. In a spreadsheet, any type of data can be held by cell, and there is a formatting toolbar or cell formatting window that makes it possible to format the cell. You can also format cells using formal cells dialog.
- **Font Name:** Through it, you can apply different font types on a worksheet.
- **Font size:** Through it, you can change the font size on a worksheet.
- **Bold:** Through it, you can make the selected text bold.
- **Italic:** Through it, you can make the selected text italicize or tilted.
- **Underline:** Through it, you can make the selected text underlined.
- **Left alignment:** Through it, you can align the text in the cell to the left.
- **Center alignment:** Through it, you can align the text in the cell to the center.
- **Right alignment:** Through it, you can align the text in the cell to the right.
- **Justify:** Through it, you can align the text in the cell to equal from left and right.
- **Increase decimal places:** It shows more precise value by showing more decimal places.
- **Decreased decimal places:** It shows less precise decimal places.
- **Merge cell:** It will merge two or more cells together.
- **Copying formula:** To speed up the process of entering the same formula to the number of cells in the rows or columns, one can do it by entering it again and again in each cell rows or columns. Another option is copying the formula and paste it in cells that results in save of time and effort when you have to enter the same long and complex formulae.
- **Relative Referencing:** By default all the cell references are relative references in which the formula gets copied in the new cell when you select any formula and drag it to new cell. There is changes in formula on the basis of relative position of rows and columns.
- **Absolute Referencing:** There are cases when you don't want a cell reference to change when copied to other cells as happen in relative referencing. In those cases absolute referencing is used as it will not change when copied and filled in another cell. To use Absolute referencing a $ symbol is used before the column name and row number that make it constant for any formula.
- **Mixed Referencing:** It is the combination of relative and absolute referencing. It is used when we have to make some row number and column name constant and some has to vary accordingly. To make the row number and column name constant a $ sign is used before it.
- **Chart:** A chart is a graphical representation of data in which the data is represented by symbols like bars in a bar chart, lines in a line chart and slices in a pie chart. You can also create charts in a tabular numeric data, function or some kind of qualitative structures. An easier way to read and data understanding is provided by charts. In MS Excel spreadsheet you can create, modify and format charts on the basis of data given in spreadsheet.

- **Column Chart:** Column charts are used for comparing several items in a specific range of values. Column charts are ideal in case of comparing a single category of data between individual sub-items such as when comparing revenue between regions. It depicts data as vertical bars.
- **Line Chart:** Line chart is one of the most frequently used chart types that is used to show trends over a period of time. It depicts data as a series of line. Mostly people consider line chart when there is need to changes chart over time.
- **Pie Chart:** Pie chart represents the distribution or proportion of each data item over a total value. It is most effective to use pie chart in plotting no more than three categories of data. It depicts data as series of slices. It is used in portray different items percentage of a store.
- **Bar Chart:** Bar charts are used for comparing several categories of data. It is ideal to be used for visualizing the distribution or proportion of data items when there are more than three categories. For instance a bar chart can be used for comparing the overall revenue distribution for a given set of products.
- **Area Chart:** Area charts are ideal for clearly illustrating the magnitude of change between two or more data points. For example you can give your audience a visual feel for the degree of variance between the high and low price of each month. It depicts a line chart whose data files in the areas between the lines and x-axis. It is mainly used in conveying the relative depth of data.
- **Scatter Chart:** Scatter charts are also known as XY scatter plot charts that are very good for showing the correlations between two sets of values. It can be used to illustrate the correlation between employee performance and competency, demonstrating that employee performance rises as competency improves. The x and y axes work together for representing data plots on the chart on the basis of intersection of x values and y values.
- **Bubble Chart:** Bubble chart is like a scatter chart with an additional third column that specifies the size of the bubbles.

■ MIND MAP

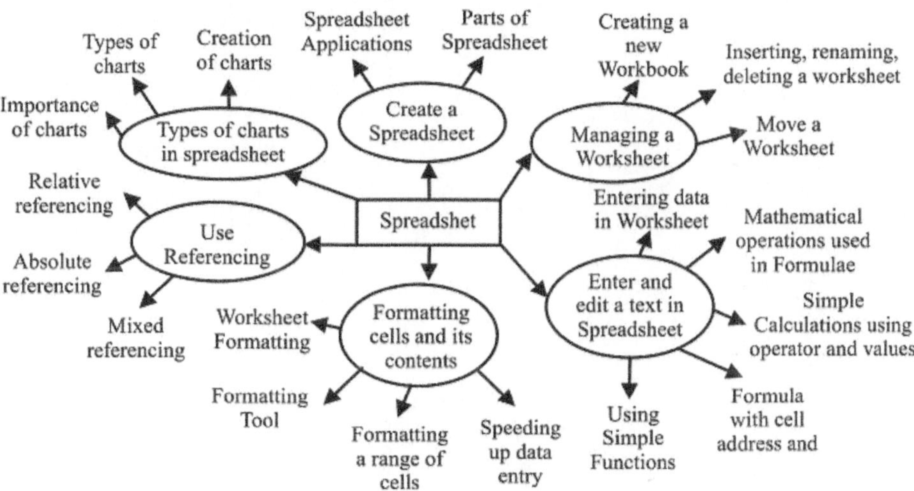

■ EXAM TIPS

1. Do all the things practically on computer to know exactly about various parts of MS Excel spreadsheet.
2. Check each parts and its further commands of MS Excel spreadsheet
3. Make a worksheet on any topic that includes label, values and formula and check everything in it like range of column, row, etc.
4. Perform different calculations both using formula and inbuilt functions.
5. Format any existing file.

5

CHAPTER

Green Skills – II

KNOWLEDGE TIPS

- The word environment has been derived from French word environ which means to surround or encircle. Its dictionary meaning is: external condition influencing growth or development of people, surrounding and working or living conditions, and more. Natural and human-made environment are two types of environment.
- An ecosystem can be defined as a functional unit of nature in which living organisms interact with each other and also with surrounding physical environment.
- Ecosystems are balanced when species coexist with other species. If something happens in an ecosystem it becomes imbalanced. Ecological imbalance takes place when a human or natural caused disturbance disrupts the natural balance of an ecosystem.
- Greenhouse gas emission, habitat distinction, radioactive wastes, nuclear weapons, overexploitation of natural resources, environmental pollution and biotechnological misuse are some of the important factors of ecological imbalance.
- Conservation is the proper management of a natural resource to prevent its exploitation, destruction or degradation. The conservation of natural resources has become necessary because of rising greed and careless attitude towards nature.
- The current strategies of economic development are using up resources of the world so rapidly that our future generations would have serious environment problems.
- Green skills are skills used for promoting green economy that are needed in areas like renewable energy, climate resilient cities, solid waste management, sewer water treatment, and green construction.
- The term Green economy was first devised in 1989 report for the Government of the United Kingdom by a group of leading environmental economists. Green economy will result in improved human well-being and social equity while reducing ecological scarcities and environmental risks.
- The three pronged approach has been proposed by United Nations Environment Programme (UNEP) for the attainment of green economy, these are low carbon growth, resource efficiency, social inclusion.
- One of the main benefits of adopting green economy is its potential to alleviate the environmental impact caused by pollution. It fights against global warming, loss of diversity and desertification.

■ TECH TIPS

- **Environment:** Environment is the sum of the total of the elements, factors and conditions in the surroundings which may have an impact on the development, action or survival of an organism or group of organisms. Biotic components: Biotic components are living components of an ecosystem. Some of these factors include animals, plants, bacteria, and fungus. On the basis of energy requirement source biotic component can be further classified.
- **Abiotic components:** Abiotic components are physical or chemical factors that act on living organisms at any part of their life. Light, soil, air, water, and minerals are form of abiotic components of an ecosystem.
- **Ecosystem:** An ecosystem can be defined as a functional unit of nature in which living organisms interact with each other and also with surrounding physical environment. Ecosystem can be as small as pond or as large as sea or forest.
- **Autotrophs:** Autotrophs are producers of energy and majority of autotrophs in an ecosystem are made by plants as they convert energy from sun or other sources into food.
- **Heterotrophs:** Heterotrophs are the consumers of energy and these organisms directly or indirectly depend upon the autotrophs of their food. They are also known as consumers and most of the heterotrophs are animals.
- **Non-living matter:** It is leaf litter, soil, sediments and other organic matter found on ground or at the bottom of an aquatic system.
- **Ecological imbalance:** Ecosystems are balanced when species coexist with other species. If something happens in an ecosystem it becomes imbalance. Ecological imbalance takes place when a human or naturally caused disturbance disrupts the natural balance of an ecosystem. Disturbance can be any changes that cause disruption in the balance of an ecosystem.
- **Greenhouse gas emission:** The greenhouse effect refers to circumstances where the short wavelength of visible light from the sun pass through a transparent medium, that is, CO, SO2, CO2, and get absorbed. But the longer wavelengths of the infrared radiation from the heated objects are unable to pass through that medium and are trapped causing more heat and a higher resultant temperature.
- **Radioactive wastes:** Nuclear reactors generate nuclear wastes and are real threat to life on Earth. Exposures to radioactive elements can have severe health effects on human being that can result in irreparable DNA damage that lead to tumors, cancers and other life threatening conditions.
- **Soil conservation:** It means checking soil erosion and improving the fertility of soil by adopting various methods that become useful in terracing, reforestation, control on grazing, etc.
- **Water conservation:** For survival of plants, mankind and animals there is a need to conserve and manage water. To achieve water conservation use the rain harvesting, grow vegetation in catchment area, Constructing dams and reservoirs, etc.
- **Reduce:** Do not use what is not required. If we reduce at source, there is a lesser chance of waste generation and the pressure on our already stretched natural resources is reduced.
- **Reuse:** Reuse the materials for other purposes, such as making pillow covers or rags out of used shirts or ladies suits.

- **Recycle:** Recycling is reusing some components of waste that may have some economic value. Recycling has readily visible benefits, such as conservation of resources, reduction in energy used during manufacturing and reduction in pollution levels.
- **Green skills:** Green skills are skills used for promoting green economy that are needed in areas like renewable energy, climate resilient cities, solid waste management, sewer water treatment and green construction. The green skills agreement defines skills for sustainability.
- **Green Economy:** A Green Economy can be thought of as an alternative vision for growth and development; one that can generate growth and improvements in people's lives in ways consistent with sustainable development. A Green Economy promotes a triple bottom line: sustaining and advancing economic, environmental and social well-being.

■ MIND MAP

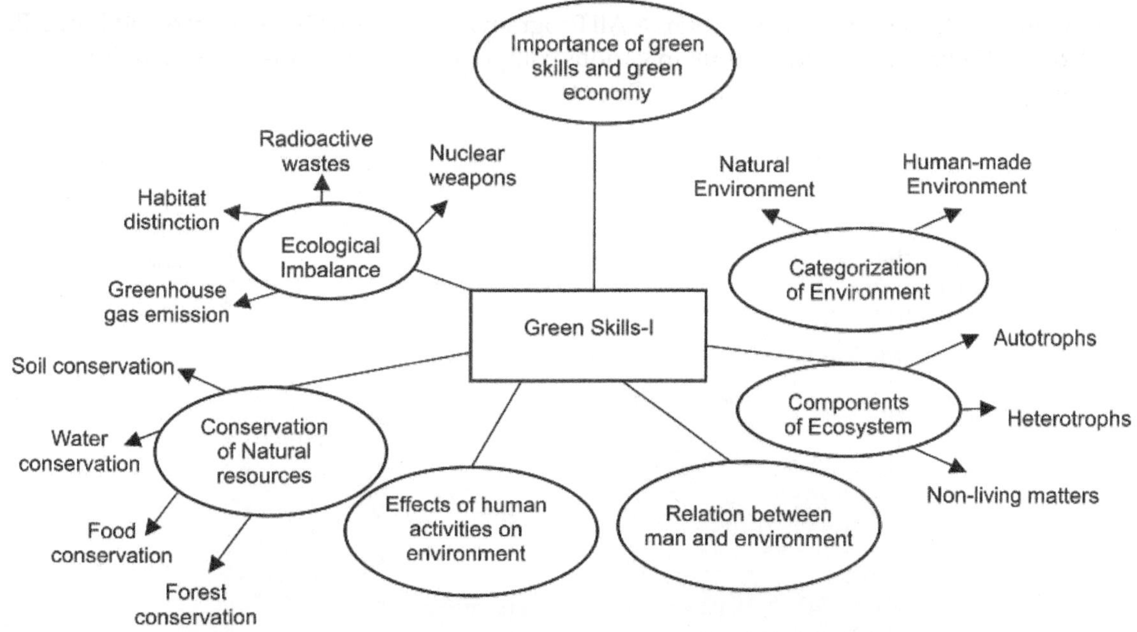

■ EXAM TIPS

1. Read the latest news on environment degradation that helps in knowing the negative effects of human and natural activities on environment. This also helps in knowing the relationship between human and environment.
2. Observe the city you are living in then make a list of biotic and abiotic components in environment.
3. Ecosystems are balanced when species coexist with other species. If something happens in an ecosystem it becomes imbalance. Make a list of things that imbalanced the ecosystem.
4. Learn the benefits of green economy by checking its importance in your surroundings.

POWERPOINT PRESENTATION

■ KNOWLEDGE TIPS

- Presentation software is used to display information in a sequence of slides or slide show that is used in colleges, schools, organizations, etc., for various purposes. MS PowerPoint is one of the presentation software that allows making dynamic slide presentations that can include images, videos, animation and text.
- Elements of Presentation are: Be prepared, Give of yourself, It has a clear objective, It's useful to your audience and Use little text in your presentation desk. While giving presentation tries to use personal examples but make sure it support your point and message you want to convey through presentation.
- To Launch a PowerPoint, Click on Start > All Programs > Microsoft Office > Microsoft PowerPoint 2010. The PowerPoint window contain various components like Tb, Title Bar, Online Tab, Ribbon, Slides pane, Notes pane, Slide, Splitter Bar, etc.

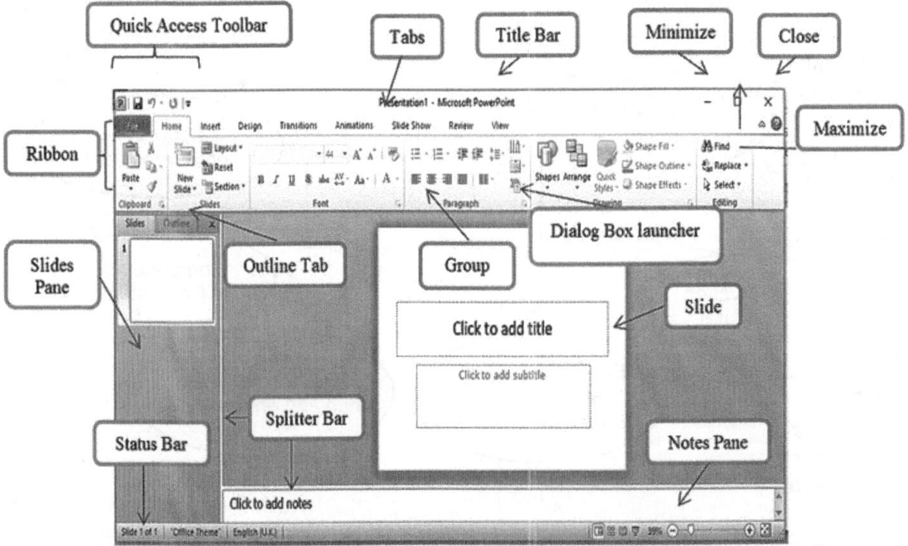

- Characteristics of good presentation are: Opening and Closing phrases, Number of lines, Font size, Use of Quotations, Correctly use grammar and language, Insert Images, clips, tables or graphs, Simplicity, Use of colours, Animation, sounds and videos, Availability of Voice and words.
- Slide is just like a paper in notebook where user can add text, image, video and audio and outline tab displays the outline of text present in each slide. The slides are present in the left part of the window. On slide user can add text, image, video and audio. It is the area in the central part of the window that is reserved for typing and adding pictures or clipart.

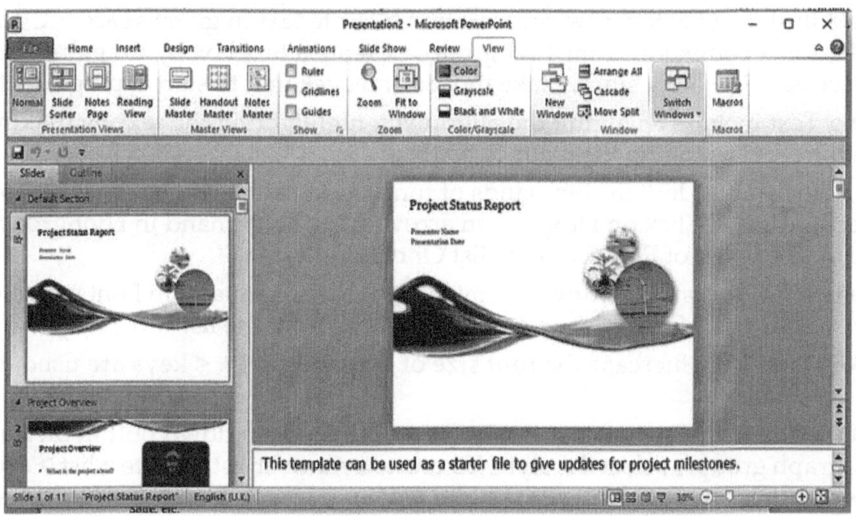

- To insert a new slide, select Slide | New Slide option. And there are a number of layouts available in Impress that can contain one or more content boxes.
- It is very time-consuming to create the same slide again and again. In Impress, there is an option to reuse the existing slide within the presentation or in any other presentation. In PowerPoint, the cut, copy, and paste operations can be done using the drag and drop method. And to use the drag and drop method, select the slide and click and hold the left mouse button on the marked slide along with the Ctrl button, move the cursor to the desired location and then release the left mouse button.
- In PowerPoint, there is a number of ways to view the created presentation. One can view the presentation in a larger size, some in a smaller size and medium size. To view the presentation in different sizes, there is an option to control the size of the view. You can control the size of the view using the zoom, and view layout dialog box opens in the view tab.
- In MS PowerPoint, we can view a presentation with different views like normal, outline, slide sorter, notes, slide master, notes master, and hand-out master. And normal view is the default type of view, and in this view, images, text, animation, video, and audio can be added on the slide.
- The thumbnail of slides is display in slides pane or a place where user can design the slides. Slide is just like a paper in notebook where user can add text, image, video and audio. Outline tab displays the outline of text present in each slide Users can type the personal notes about the current slide in notes pane.
- To Close PowerPoint, Select the File Menu > Exit option.
- To select a slide layout, Select Slide Menu > Slide Layout > Title slide.
- To Save a Presentation, Select File Menu > Save option
- To Save a presentation with different name, Select File > Save As
- To run a Slide Show, Click on Slide Show > Select Start from Fist Slide on the main menu bar
- To Close a Presentation, Select File Menu > Close option
- Formatting is the change of appearance of text by changing font color, size and style.

- To add text in slide, Create a new presentation > Write text in given space > Click on Insert Tab > Select Text Box command from Text group > Create a text box by dragging the mouse on the slide then release it > Now simply take mouse and click in it to start typing a text
- Formatting Text include changing the alignment, highlighting the text by making it bold, italic and underline and changing the color of textbox
- The bold, italic and underline commands of font group can be added in slide. To change font of Text, Select the text > Click on Drop down arrow of Font command in Font group of home tab > Select the desired type of Font from the list Or click
- Select the text > Click on Drop down arrow of Font Size command in Font group of home tab Or press Ctrl + Shift + P > Select the desired size of Font from the list
- Ctrl + > key is used to increase the font size of text and Ctrl + < keys are used to decrease size of text
- To add Bullets in text, Create a list > select it > click on drop down button on Bullets command from paragraph group > select the style. To create a number list, Create a list > select it > click on drop down button on Numbering command from paragraph group > select the style
- To apply shadow effect, Select the Text > Click on Text Shadow button given in Font group of Home tab
- MS PowerPoint enables the user to add tables in the slides for representation of statistical data meaningfully. Table is a grid of cells arranged in rows and columns format. To enter the data in a table, place the insertion point in a required cell then start typing text or data you want to enter in it.
- To select a cell within a table, Position the mouse cursor along with its left edge then press right mouse button when the cursor changes to a sloped white arrow To select a row or column within a table, Press right mouse button on the row or column you want to select > Select option from the context menu. To select an entire table, Click on the edge of table > Click on the left mouse button when the mouse cursor changes to a slopped arrow.
- To adjust column width, Position on the border line between two columns > Press the left mouse button when the cursor position changes to both side arrow sign > Drag it until column comes to desired width. To adjust Row height, Position on the border line between two rows > Press the left mouse button when the cursor position changes to both side arrow sign > Drag it until row comes to desired height.
- To apply Border to the Table, Right click on the border of table > Click on Table Properties dialog box will open > Now click on Border tab > Do the needful changes in the borders. To delete a Table, Click on the Table > Select it > Press Delete key button on the keyboard.
- In PowerPoint you can insert graphics or images from the gallery, files stored in the computer, etc. The pictures can be added in slide from saved pictures in your system of different formats.
- To move the inserted image, Click on Image > wait till the cursor changes to hand shape > Click on image and drag it to the desired position > Release the mouse button
- To resize the image, Click on Image > Put the cursor on one of the selection handles on the image and the cursor will change the shape by giving a graphical representation of the direction of the resizing > Click and drag the image to resize it > Release the mouse button.
- To rotate the Image, Click on Image > Click on Rotate icon on the Line and Filling toolbar > Click again on the selected image and shape and colour of selection handles get changed > Click the mouse and move it in the required direction > Release the mouse button.

- Instead of formatting manually, you can also format the image using Image toolbar. It comes under properties window after selecting the image in the slide.
- In PowerPoint there are number of drawing tools that have various tools for creating graphical objects. To draw a line in a slide of PowerPoint, Click on Insert Menu bar > Click on shapes command > Select the desired from the available line option.
- To draw a shape in slide of PowerPoint, Click on Insert Menu bar > Click on shapes command > Select the desired from the available shape option. In PowerPoint you can draw various shapes then group all the objects to a single object. To ungroup the object, Select the group > Right click on it > Select Ungroup option from context menu.
- PowerPoint comes with five prepacked slide masters. These are shown in the Master Pages section of the Tasks Pane or Sidebar. All the slide masters in Available for Use list is from a template of the same name. This list also contains your own created templates or templates added from other sources, slide masters from those templates.
- You can also create your own slide master like modifying the default slide master. To enable editing of a slide master, Select View menu bar > Master Slide. To open the slide Transition section, Click on the Slide Transition icon available in Sidebar.
- To apply transition to all the slides, Select the slides from Slides pane or Slide Sorter view to apply the transition to all the slides. To select a transition, Select a transition in the Apply to selected slides list. To play the sound during transitions, Select a sound from Sound list.

■ TECH TIPS

- **Presentation:** A presentation is a means of communication that can be adapted to various speaking situations, such as talking to a group, addressing a meeting or briefing a team.
- **Opening and Closing phrases:** The opening and closing of presentation means carefully framed by keeping in view the situation, subject and audience.
- **PowerPoint:** PowerPoint is a Microsoft presentation program that creates a slide show of important information, charts, and images to display during a presentation. It is most often used for business and school presentations.
- **Animation:** It controls the order and style that objects will enter or exit from the slide
- **Design:** Controls the overall look and feel of your presentation with theme and style settings.
- **Spelling and Grammar Check:** Grammar and spelling help to run a spelling and grammar check in your presentation.
- **Title Bar:** On top and middle of word window there is title bar. Both the name of program and its currently used presentation is display on it.
- **Quick access toolbar:** It is located in the top left side of title bar which is used for common buttons such as Redo, Undo and save.
- **Ribbon:** The ribbon menu is found across many of Microsoft's apps, such as Word, Excel, and PowerPoint. It lives above the main area of the application.
- **Window Management Buttons:** Window management buttons includes the Minimizer, Maximize or restore and Close window management buttons. Each have their own functioning as to hide buttons from desktop screen a minimize button is used and to enlarge window back to its standard size a maximize button is used and to close application a Close button is used.

- **Slides:** The slides are present in the left part of the window. On slide user can add text, image, video and audio.
- **Slides Pane:** The thumbnail of slides is display in slides pane or a place where user can design the slides. It allow user to add new slides, remove or rearrange slides.
- **Outline Tab:** It displays the outline of text present in each slide and in this view user can directly edit their text.
- **Notes Pane:** Users can type the personal notes about the current slide in notes pane and these notes do not appear on the screen in slide show mode.
- **Splitter Bar:** The size of panes can be adjusted using these two horizontal and vertical bars.
- **Layouts:** In PowerPoint you can also prepare ypu own layput and safe it for future use.
- **Status Bar:** Status bar gives the working document status like slide number, Name of theme, Spell check, View and Zoom slider options.
- **Custom Animation:** In a slide there are various custom animation features for drawings, text, etc., through which you can add, change or remove animation features.
- **Zoom Control:** It help in changing the scale of the text and pictures in the document for view. It does not affect the physical document.
- **Slide Layout:** Slide layouts are used PowerPoint which can contain one or more content boxes. In these content boxes we can insert images, charts, movies, tables, sound, text, etc.
- **Copying and Moving Slides:** To move the slide to another location or to reuse it use the cut and paste and copy and paste process respectively.
- **View a Presentation:** we can view the presentation in larger size, some in smaller size and medium size. So, as per the requirements we can view the presentation in different sizes.
- **Slide Layout:** There are number of layouts available in PowerPoint that can contains one or more content boxes. In these content boxes you can insert images, charts, movies, tables, sound, text, etc. On the basis of content you want to add, you can select the icon.
- **Backspace and Delete:** There is a difference in the Delete and Backspace button. As the delete button will delete the content from the right of the corner, on the other hand, the Backspace key or button will delete from the left of the corner. Pressing any of the Delete or Backspace key will delete one character at a time.
- **View a Presentation:** In PowerPoint there are number of ways to view the created presentation. One can view the presentation in larger size, some in smaller size and medium size. So, as per user requirements one can view the presentation in different sizes.
- **Workspace Views:** In MS PowerPoint we can view a presentation with different views like Normal, Slide Sorter, Notes Page and Slide show. The default view of PowerPoint 2010 is Normal view.
- **Normal View:** This is the default type of view and in this view images, text, animation, video and audio can be added on slide. User can see Slide pane, Notes pane and left pane that have Outline and Slide tab.
- **Slide Sorter View:** using Slide sorter view, user will get the miniature view of all the slides that is mainly helpful in rearranging, deleting, changing order of slides, adding translation, setting the timings for the slide show and adding a new slide, etc.
- **Slide Show View:** This view is used to give presentation to another person. By clicking on this view a presentation will start either from first or current slide one after another in defined

sequence. The entire screen is occupied by single slide that helps in seeing how your animation, movies, timings graphics and transition effects look in actual show.

- **Reading View:** It is similar to slide show view as in both slide is shown in full screen mode. The only difference in reading view is that title bar and status bar is displayed in it. This view helps in easily navigate during slide show as in slide show view along with that it provides an easy access to window task bar to switch to other open window or programs.
- **Notes Page view:** This will give the Note page for particular slide to edit the speaker notes information which is not visible to other person while giving presentation. This will help speaker in remembering the important points to discuss and giving to audience.
- **Slide Show:** Control settings related to the way your presentation appears when sharing it with an audience.
- **Adding Text:** The text can be added in slide by simply clicking on it and start typing. In case to add more text than the area provided for entering text user can insert a text box.
- **Formatting Text:** User can also edit text in presentation like changing the alignment, highlighting the text by making it bold, italic and underline and changing the color of textbox.
- **Align Text:** It is related to the position of text in the slide. There can be four ways or option to align a text.
- **Align Text left:** The left text alignment is a default type of alignment. In this case there is little space in the right side. Click on Align Text left command given in Paragraph group of Home tab or Shortcut key (Ctrl + L)
- **Center:** This will align the text in the center of document and leave little space from both the ends. Mainly its use has been found in writing the title. Click on Center command given in Paragraph group of Home tab or Shortcut key (Ctrl + E)
- **Align Text Right:** This is the opposite case of left text alignment as in this the text is align towards right side and leave little space in the left. Mainly used to put sign and date option or sometimes giving the chapter heading. Click on Align Text right command given in Paragraph group of Home tab or Shortcut key (Ctrl + R)
- **Justify:** In this case text is evenly aligned between the left and right side. Click on Justify command given in Paragraph group of Home tab or Shortcut key (Ctrl + J)
- **Drawing graphic objects:** In PowerPoint, there are number of drawing tools that have various tools for creating graphical objects.
- **Bullets:** Mainly unordered list are created using bullet as there is no sequence of items in it. There are various styles of bullets available in PowerPoint.
- **Numbering:** Mainly ordered list are created using number as there is sequence of items in it. There are various styles of numbering available in PowerPoint.
- **Inserting pictures from files:** The pictures can be added in slide from saved pictures in your system of different formats. The pictures can be of JPG, BMP, PNG, JPEG and GIF format.
- **Inserting Images from the Internet:** Sometimes there are cases when image is not present in system or you don't want to add clip art. In those cases images are taken from Internet.
- **Formatting Images:** We have learnt to insert an image but sometimes there can be requirements of formatting that image such as moving, resizing, rotating, etc. Various formatting on inserted images are moving images, resizing images and Rotating it.

- **Drawing graphic objects:** PowerPoint there are number of drawing tools that have various tools for creating graphical objects.
- **Grouping Objects:** There are some cases in which we have to use various shapes to create flowchart, figure, etc. In those cases you can draw various shapes then group all the objects to a single object.
- **Ungrouping Objects:** There are some cases in which you have to insert any new object in grouped objects. In those cases there is option of ungroup objects in Impress.
- **Slide Master:** A slide master controls the overall appearance, such as formatting and design, of each slide layout, and therefore each slide in your presentation. When you modify the slide master within your presentation, the changes will be applied to every slide layout. All templates contain at least one slide master.

■ MIND MAP

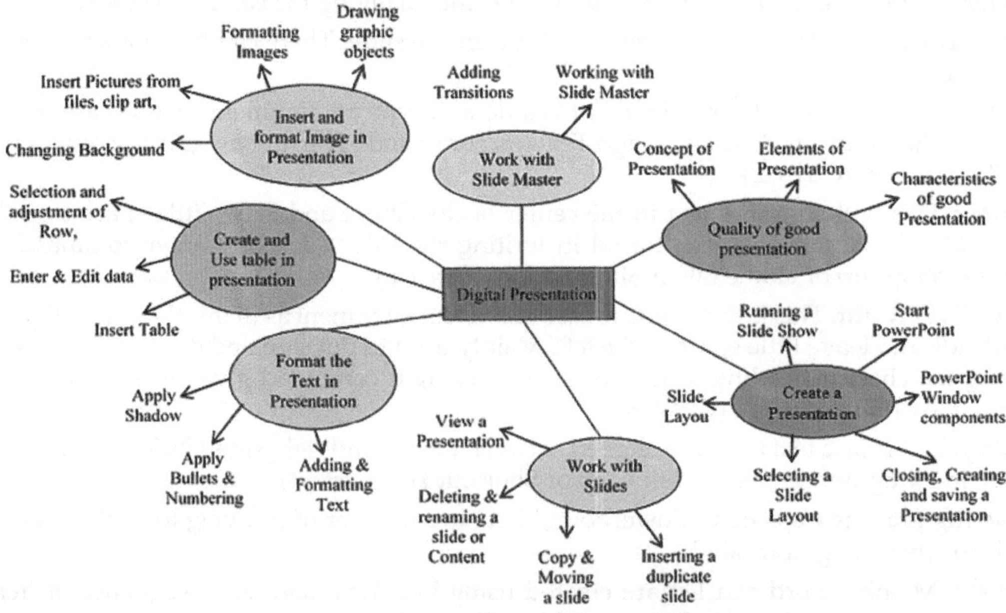

■ EXAM TIPS

1. Keep in mind the elements and characteristics of good quality presentation in mind while making a presentation.
2. Perform every task practically.
3. Check the operation of each element of PowerPoint window while reading it at your home or lab.
4. Save a presentation in pdf to learn the steps to perform it.
5. Physically check the difference of various workspace views available in PowerPoint.

Solved Sample Papers

INFORMATION TECHNOLOGY (402)

Solved Sample Paper – 1

M.M. 50 **Time: 2 hrs**

General Instructions:

i. Read the question paper carefully.

ii. Question Paper is divided into four sections.

Attempt any of 10 questions from this section:

- **Section A: Multiple choice questions (1 marks each)**

  Attempt any of 6 questions from this section.

- **Section B: Very short Answer (2 marks each)**

  All questions are compulsory in these sections.

- **Section C: Short Answer (3 marks each)**
- **Section D: Long Answer (5 marks each)**

Section A: Multiple Choice Questions (1 marks each)

1. What is the purpose of the receiver in communication?

   a. Understand the message and respond to it

   b. Send message c. Take response

   d. None

2. ____________ phase of entrepreneurship development includes all the activities and preparation required to launch a training program.

3. ____________ is a form of BPM that is a cost-saving technique which involves contracting business tasks to a third party.

   a. IT b. BPO

   c. ITeS d. None

4. To operate or press a key on the fourth or number row use:

   a. Ring finger type 1 b. Ring finger type 2

   c. Ring finger type 3 d. Ring finger type 4

5. Save and Save As perform same task. (T/F)

6. Which of the following is the shortcut key to close Impress?

   a. Ctrl + Q b. Alt + Q

   c. Shift + Q d. Ctrl + N

7. ___________ is not a display on Status bar.
   a. Slide number b. Name of theme
   c. Slide Style d. Spell check
8. Title bar exist on ___________ and middle of excel window.
9. The frequently used common buttons are present on ___________.
10. The title bar in PowerPoint contains Presentation name and name of application. (T/F)

Section B: Very Short Questions (2 marks each)

1. Give various characteristics of Entrepreneurship.
2. Name components of CPU.
3. Name various View option in PowerPoint?
4. What is the need of copying a text?
5. Define Floating Toolbar?

   Or

   What is Page Break?
6. Explain the role of the navigation tree in the Lesson editor.
7. What is the importance of Charts in Spreadsheet?
8. Give various elements of Presentation?

Section C: Short Questions (3 marks each)

1. How to check spelling and grammar mistakes using Synonyms and Thesaurus?
2. Give various processes of workplace where IT is used.
3. Give various mathematical operators used in Formulae with example.
4. Give a brief about various paragraph alignment styles in MS Word.
5. Is it possible to insert a duplicate slide in PowerPoint? If Yes, then write down the steps to insert a duplicate slide in it.
6. What is Mixed Referencing?

Section D: Long Questions (5 marks each)

1. Write down the steps and options of moving and copying the text in MS Word?
2. Write a short note of speeding up data entry using Fill handle?

ANSWERS

Section A

1. a	2. Pre-training or Initial phase	3. b	4. b	5. False
6. a	7. c	8. Top	9. Quick Access Toolbar	10. True

Section B

1. Various characteristics of Entrepreneurship are:
   - It is a function of Innovation
   - It is a function of leadership
   - It is an Organization building function
   - It involves operation and creation of an enterprise
   - It is concerned with managing, developing and employing the factors of production
2. CPU consists of Arithmetic Logic Unit, Memory Unit and Control Unit.
3. In MS PowerPoint we can view a presentation with different views like Normal, Outline, Slide Sorter, Notes, Slide Master, Notes Master and Handout Master.
4. If you want to create or use the same data, then copy command of MS Word 2010 can be used. Either single or multiple copies of data can be created by using single command without affecting the existing data. This will save time and efforts that user has to put in writing the same data again in different location.
5. The floating toolbar is just below the Standard Toolbar. It is context sensitive that shows the tools relevant to the current position of the cursor or the selected object.

   Or

   Page break is also known as hard page break that is a code inserted by a software program like LibreOffice Writer that tells the printing device where to end the current page and begin the next. It will move the text to a new page before reaching the end of page.
6. In the navigation tree, student properties and a group of selected items can be edited.
7. Importance of Charts in Spreadsheet are:
   - As mentioned above the visual representation of data is preferred in case of large amount of data. That's why a charts are introduced in every spreadsheet.
   - It is not easy to compare and analyse data when they are represented as numbers in large quantity
   - The data in the form of charts are more effective in communication and understanding
   - You can create charts in tabular numeric data, function or some kind of qualitative structures
8. Various Elements of presentation that makes it effective are:
   - Be Prepared
   - Give of Yourself
   - Stay Relaxed
   - It has a clear objective
   - It's useful to your audience
   - Use little text in your presentation desk

Section C

1. The synonyms, antonyms, word substitute, and alternative spelling comes in word through thesaurus. Both dictionary and thesaurus are different from each other as there is synonyms, antonyms in thesaurus on other hand dictionary contains pronunciation and definitions. Synonyms are a word having a similar meaning to the word you have enter. On other hand antonyms are words option with opposite meaning of typed word. Thesaurus help users while writing by giving suggestions to make them to better understand their words. To use thesaurus, follow the steps:

   Select the word > right click on it > click on synonyms from the context menu

   The selected word or phrase will be highlighted in the document and will get same meaning word for selected word.
2. Technology is such an integral part of 21-st century workplace that any business without some level of technical knowledge will fail. In workplaces or offices, computer and its applications are used to perform work more effectively that makes computer use as prevalent. Some offices or companies may find functioning without them is virtually impossible.
3. In Excel or spreadsheet software there is most powerful features by which user can calculate numerical data by applying various formulae. Formulas are simply equations that perform calculations on values in our sheet. This can include numbers, parenthesis, cell address and arithmetic operators and result will be displayed on the cell where user has entered the formula.

Operation	Symbol Name	Symbol	Example
Addition	Plus sign	+	B2+C2, B3+6
Subtraction	Minus sign	-	B2-C2
Multiplication	Asterisk	*	C2*D2
Division	Forward slash	/	C2/D2

4. The position of paragraph between the page margins is known as paragraph alignment. By default the text is align in left side of the document and the right margins in the document is known as horizontal text alignment.

   There are mainly four paragraph alignment styles comes under this category are:
   - **Align Paragraph left:** The left Paragraph alignment is a default type of alignment. In this case there is little space in the right side.
   - **Center:** This will align the Paragraph in the center of document and leave little space from both the ends. Mainly its use has been found in writing the title.
   - **Align Paragraph Right:** This is the opposite case of left Paragraph alignment as in this the Paragraph is align towards right side and leave little space in the left. Mainly used to put sign and date option or sometimes giving the chapter heading.

     Justify: In this case Paragraph is evenly aligned between the left and right side.
5. Yes, You can insert a duplicate slide in PowerPoint.

To insert a duplicate slide, perform the following steps and using the options given below:
Select the slide from Slide Pane > Select Slide menu bar > Duplicate Slide

OR

Another option is: Right click on the slide > Select Duplicate Slide from the menu

6. Mixed is the combination of relative and absolute referencing. It is used when we have to make some row number and column name constant and some has to vary accordingly. To make the row number and column name constant a $ sign is used before it.

   For example: We have entered the number of class 9th students in English, =hindi, maths and IT subject. In Total marks we have taken the sum in which the relative referencing is used as arguments cell name is varying according to their position. Same is for average but in GR total column you can observe that the Sum column is varying and grace marks column name is constant and $ sign is added before the row number. This shows the mixed referencing.

Section D

1. If you want to create or use the same data, then copy command of MS Word can be used. Either single or multiple copies of data can be created by using single command without affecting the existing data. This will save time and efforts that user have to put in writing the same data again in different location. The copy operation can be done by performing following steps:

   Copy and Paste: It is used when you want the duplicate copy of the selected text. To perform copy and paste, perform the following steps:

   Step 1: Select the text > Click on Edit menu > Click on Copy option

   Or

   Another option to Copy the text is select the text > Right click on it > Select Copy option

2. In MS Excel Fill Handle tool you can fill the next cells by dragging it with the next predefined value. For example you want to fill the Roll numbers, Month, Week, Days, etc., then you can input one or two in sequence then select them and drag it to the next cell or till that you want to continue that series of sequence.

   - **For number series:** To speed up the process of entering number series, perform the following steps:
   - Type numbers 1, 2 in two consecutive cells > Select them using mouse > Click on right down corner of the last selected cell and drag it downward till that you want to continue the number series. You can also get a series on different interval by giving the difference between two consecutive cell values then drag them downward.
   - **Copying Formula:** To speed up the process of entering the same formula to the number of cells in the rows or columns one option is to enter it again and again in each cell rows or columns. Other option is copying the formula and paste it in cells that results in save of time and efforts when you have to enter the same long and complex formulae.
   - **Various Options to Copying a Formula and using it are:** Use of copy and paste commands: In this you just have to select the cell contain formula then select the cell on which you want to enter that same formula. Now Press Paste command to paste that same formula in selected cell.

INFORMATION TECHNOLOGY (402)

Solved Sample Paper – 2

M.M. 50 **Time: 2 hrs**

General Instructions:

i. Read the question paper carefully.

ii. Question Paper is divided into four sections.

Attempt any of 10 questions from this section:

- **Section A: Multiple choice questions (1 marks each)**
  Attempt any of 6 questions from this section.
- **Section B: Very short Answer (2 marks each)**
  All questions are compulsory in these sections.
- **Section C: Short Answer (3 marks each)**
- **Section D: Long Answer (5 marks each)**

Section A: Multiple Choice Questions (1 marks each)

1. Which of the following is a Volatile memory?

   a. ROM b. Internal

   c. External d. RAM

2. PowerPoint presentations are widely used as

   a. note outlines for teachers

   b. project presentations by students

   c. communication of planning d. All of above

3. Entrepreneur is a self-employed person who is willing to take risk and start a business with new idea (T/F)

4. Verbal communication involves

   a. Any message that uses words of different languages

   b. A written message

   c. A Spoken message

   d. Both b and c

5. To cancel the last editing ____________ button is used.

6. The range of normal human hearing is in the range of
   a. 10 Hz to 80 Hz
   b. 50 Hz to 80 Hz
   c. 50 Hz to 15000 Hz
   d. 15000 Hz and above
7. The fingertips of your left hand should always be placed on these keys:
   a. Q, w, e, r
   b. A, s, d, f
   c. A, d, g, i
   d. A, d, f, g
8. How do you delete a column?
   a. Select the column heading you want to delete and select the Delete Row button on the standard toolbar
   b. Select the column heading you want to delete and select Insert Delete from the menu
   c. Select the row heading you want to delete and select Edit>Delete from the menu
   d. Right click the column heading you want to delete and select delete from the shortcut menu
9. The Green color in summary indicates:
   a. Right inputs
   b. Wrong inputs exceed the acceptable timeframe
   c. Wrong inputs within the acceptable timeframe
   d. Right inputs exceeding the acceptable timeframe
10. In order to edit a chart, you can
    a. Triple click the chart object
    b. Click and drag the chart object
    c. Double click the chart object
    d. Click the chart object

Section B: Very Short Questions (2 marks each)

1. Name applications of word processing?
2. Define standard toolbar?
3. What do you mean by self-confidence?

   Or

   What do you mean by visual communication?
4. What is a worksheet? How one can insert more worksheet?
5. Explain Mobile as ICT tool?
6. Define mouse used in computer system?
7. What is the function of Alt key?
8. Define the usage of Average in Excel? Give example.

Section C: Short Questions (3 marks each)

1. Write a note on entering data in worksheet including various types of data one can enter in it.
2. Write a short note on entrepreneurship development?

3. Give in detail about checking spelling and grammar in the document types in Word processor?
4. Give various types of text alignment option in detail with their shortcuts?
5. Write a note on Internal and External memory?
6. Define Home row keys and Guide keys?

Section D: Long Questions (5 marks each)

1. Give in detail about various parts of MS Excel?
2. What is the purpose of Bullets and Number list in presentation? Give the definition of both along with the steps to insert it in the slides.

ANSWERS

Section A

1. d	2. d	3. True	4. d	5. Undo
6. c	7. b	8. d	9. a	10. c

Section B

1. Various word processing applications are:
   - WordPad
   - Microsoft Word
   - Google Docs
   - Notepad
   - OpenOffice Writer
   - LibreOffice Writer
2. The standard toolbar is just under the menu bar, and it is also known as a docked or fixed toolbar. It consists of command in the form of icons and is consistent across the Microsoft Office applications.
3. Self-confidence is a sense of trusting one's own abilities. If you are a hardworking, talented and intelligent person but have lack of confidence and don't take initiatives then other people will be unable to recognize your talent.

   Or

   In visual communication, a message is delivered using words as it is the most powerful and accurate tools in expressing and sharing ideas.
4. Worksheet is a grid that consists of a number of rows and columns in which data is entered by a user. By default, there is a single worksheet in Excel , name Sheet1displayed at the bottom left side. In the case of working with huge data, further sheets can be added in it by clicking on the insert worksheet button + sign given before the default sheet.

5. Earlier time, it was used for calls, but nowadays, it is loaded with various applications to complete tasks in few times. Like Paytm wallet and Google pay for money transfer, WhatsApp for messaging, Games, and many more can be downloaded in it.
6. The mouse, sometimes called a pointer, is a hand-operated input device used to manipulate objects on a computer screen. Whether the mouse uses a laser or ball, or is wired or wireless, a movement detected from the mouse sends instructions to the computer to move the cursor on the screen in order to interact with files, windows, and other software elements.
7. Alt key stands for Alternate that is press together with another ley so that the other key does something different from what it usually does. It is like a second control key.
8. The arithmetic mean and an average of the arguments is returned by the AVERAGE function. In arguments, users can enter the range of cells, direct numbers, both numbers, and cell reference. For example:
   - AVERAGE(B2:B6)
   - AVERAGE(B2,B6)

Section C

1. In MS Excel, there is a need to select the cell before entering data in the worksheet or cell. To select a cell, simply position the pointer in that particular cell. You can enter a label, values, or formula data in the any cell.
   - **Label:** It is any text that can be letters, numbers, and special symbols that entered using the keyboard. By default, labels are aligned on the left side.
   - **Values:** It is the numeric data consists of only numbers. By defaults, they are aligned on the right side. Various forms of values are integer, decimal, and more.
   - **Formulae:** It is the expression that begins with an equals (=) sign. The formula is always started by= and followed by values, cell addresses, and functions. After entering the formula in a cell, then the value of the equation is displayed in the cell, and the formulas bar contains the formula.
   - **Values:** It is the numeric data consists of only numbers. By defaults, they are aligned on the right side. Various forms of values are integer, decimal, and more.
   - Formulae: It is the expression that begins with an equals (=) sign. The formula is always started by= and followed by values, cell addresses, and functions. After entering the formula in a cell, then the value of the equation is displayed in the cell, and the formulas bar contains the formula.
2. It is the process of improving the skills and knowledge of entrepreneurs through various training and classroom programs.

   For example: To score good in examinations, students go for extra classes or coaching and also to improve their communication skills they join various English communication courses and personality grooming institutes.

   In the same way entrepreneurship development is the process to enhance one's personality and take them a step forward toward success. It is mainly concerned with the study of entrepreneurial behavior, the dynamics of business set-up, development and expansion of the enterprise. The main objective is to increase the number of entrepreneurs.

3. Errors are related to spelling and grammar mistakes. In LibreOffice, there is a built-in feature of checking and correcting the errors. It helps in correcting the spelling as well as grammar. You can use both separately or in combination with each other. You will observe the different colors of the line for a different type of mistake in your text.

- **Blue wavy line:** The blue line will come under the word or sentence if there are grammatical errors in the text. These types of errors can be removed by right-clicking on it and selecting the right option. In the context menu that comes after right-clicking on the blue wavy line, the first entry gives the name of suspected grammatical error, and in the second entry, it gives suggestions for correction. The spelling checker checks for spelling mistakes in the typed text or words that are not present in the installed dictionary list.
- **Red wavy line or spelling mistake:** The red wavy line highlights the errors related to spelling mistakes. In case, if you found a red line under your text, then right-click on the text that has a red wavy line and select the matching word.

4. It is related to the position of text in the slide. There can be four ways or option to align a text:
    - **Align text left:** The left text alignment is a default type of alignment. In this case, there is little space on the right side. Click on the Format tab | Align option. Click on the Left, and the shortcut key is (Ctrl + L).
    - **Center:** This will align the text in the center of the slide and leave little space from both the ends. Mainly its use has been found in writing the title. Click on the Format tab | Align option. Click on the Center or shortcut key (Ctrl + E).
    - **Align text right:** This is the opposite case of left text alignment as in this, the text is aligned towards the right side and leaves little space in the left. Click on the Format tab | Align option. Click on the Right or shortcut key (Ctrl + R).
5. Internal and external are two categories of computer memory:
    - **Internal memory:** The default memory of a computer is known as internal memory, main memory, or primary memory. In primary memory, programs or instructions are stored temporarily. It is fast in speed; that's why it is known as immediate access storage but has a very little capacity of storage.

      Random-access memory (RAM) and Read-only memory (ROM) are two internal memories that hold the data temporarily. RAM is volatile in nature as it lost data when the power supply is switched off. On the other hand, ROM is non-volatile, and data and instructions saved in ROM are not lost by switching off the power supply.
    - **External memory:** It is also known as secondary or auxiliary memory and used due to expensive, temporary, and less storage capacity of internal memory. So that when required, the data can be transferred to external memory from internal memory. It orders to make data permanent; it is used in a secondary storage device that makes it accessible for a long time. The disadvantage of external memory is its low speed.

      Example: CD/DVD, hard disks, pen drive, and more.
6. The home keys are the row of keys on the computer keyboard; your fingers rest on when not typing. The Alphabets ASDF are home keys for left hand and LKJ along with semi-colon (;) are for the right hand. For both hands, the thumb rests on the spacebar.

   By positioning your hands correctly on the home row keys, you can memorize where all other keys on the keyboard are located. If your fingers are trained to make the correct movement to other keys, and after that, it returns to their respective home key, and then you will be able to type in fast speed.

The guide keys are those keys that help in moving the cursor using the keyboard. On a computer keyboard, the F key for the left hand and J key for the right hand are guide keys. This helps touch typists in placing the fingers correctly on home keys.

Section D

1. Various parts of MS Excel are:

   Title Bar: On top and middle of excel window there is title bar. Both the name of program and its currently used document name is display on it. It also contains minimize, maximize and Close buttons.

   Quick access toolbar: It is located in the top left side of title bar. The frequently used common buttons are present on it. Redo, Undo and save are three buttons that are present by default on it. We can remove or add other button through the drop down arrow present on it

   Tabs: Below the title bar there is tabs that contains various group of command used to work in word. Some of the tabs in excel are home, insert, page layout, formulas, Data, review, view.

   Ribbon: On clicking of any tab a ribbon appears. It contains tab, groups and commands. On top of ribbon button there are 7 tabs that contains groups of related commands. All related commands are organized in groups. As shown the figure the font contains its group of commands, clipboard contains commands related to it, etc. Within each group there are commands. By default the home tab appears after launching the word.

   Name Box: Active cell name is present in Name box that is located on left side before the Formula box in top of worksheet.

   Formula Bar: In formula bar user can directly enter the formulae or data or click on cell that contains formula then it will start appearing on formula bar. It is located in right side of Name box.

   Scrollbar: It helps in page down or up and left or right the work window by which we can check the not visible part on the window. There are two types of scrollbars name as horizontal and vertical. The horizontal bar helps in navigating from left to right and it is present in bottom above the status bar. Other type is vertical bar that is present in right and used to navigate the document from top to bottom.

   Status Bar: Below the horizontal scrollbar there is status bar that gives working worksheet status like sheet number, active working mode, zoom functioning along with other spreadsheet related important information.

   Sheet Tabs: The sheet tabs are available on left bottom side of excel file. By defaults there are three sheets name as Sheet1, Sheet2 and Sheet3. The particular worksheet become active by clicking on it from bottom sheet tabs. More sheets can be added in it by clicking on inserting worksheet given next to Sheet3. The name of these sheets can be changed by right click on name of particular sheet and selecting rename option or by double clicking on name and entering the required name in it.

   Quick access toolbar: It is located on the top left side of the title bar. The frequently used common buttons are present on it. We can remove or add another button through the drop-down arrow present on it.

Toolbars: There are by default two toolbars in Calc that provide a wide range of common commands and functions. A tooltip or small box is displayed by placing the mouse cursor over any icon.

- **Standard toolbar:** It shows the icons for most common operations such as editing, arranging, filtering, and more.
- **Formatting toolbar:** It consists of most common operations related to datasheet formatting such as font selection, size of text, alignment, cell value formatting and indentation, and more.

Control buttons: On the top right side of the Title bar, there are control buttons such as minimize, maximize, and close.

Column and row heading: The column and row heading are the names of rows and columns.

Active cell: A thick black color boundary appears on the cell when we click on it that makes it different from non-active cells. Users can enter or edit data only inactive cells. The name given to this highlighted box is the cell pointer.

2. To put a list of items in a good manner format, there is an option of bullet and numbering in Impress. These both will arrange the content in the form of lists. Both options are there in the Format tab. There is a various style of bullet and number available in Impress.

Bullet: Mainly unordered list are created using bullet as there is no sequence of items in it. There are various styles of bullets available in Impress. Different ways to create a bullet list:

- Create a list and select it. Click on Format tab | Lists | Bulleted List option.
- Click on Toggle Bullet list | More Bullets | Bullets and Numbering dialog box will appear

The Bullets and Numbering dialog box contain various options. You can select any of the options of bullets given in the dialog box.

When you select the style of the bullet it will start appearing on the selected text in the slide. Now, if you want to use the bullet on another typed document, then simply take cursor on the last text with a bullet, press enter, and write the text or list. To stop bullet options, simply again click on it and start typing.

Numbering: Mainly ordered list are created using the number as there is a sequence of items in it. There are various styles of numbering available in Impress:

- Create a list and select it. Click on Format tab | Lists | Numbered List option.
- Click on Toggle Numbered list | More Bullets | Bullets and Numbering dialog box will appear

When you select the style of the number, it will appear on the selected text on the slide. Now, if you want to continue with count on another typed document, then simply take cursor on last numbered text, press enter, and write the text or list. To stop the numbering option, simply again click on it and start typing.

INFORMATION TECHNOLOGY (402)

Solved Sample Paper – 3

M.M. 50 **Time: 2 hrs**

General Instructions:

i. Read the question paper carefully.

ii. Question Paper is divided into four sections.

Attempt any of 10 questions from this section:

- **Section A: Multiple choice questions (1 marks each)**
  Attempt any of 6 questions from this section.
- **Section B: Very short Answer (2 marks each)**
  All questions are compulsory in these sections.
- **Section C: Short Answer (3 marks each)**
- **Section D: Long Answer (5 marks each)**

Section A: Multiple Choice Questions (1 marks each)

1. What is the use of bookmarks in Microsoft Word?
   a. To easily correct the spelling error
   b. To quickly jump to a specific location in the document
   c. To quickly jump to the ending of the document
   d. To create a link within the document
2. People with self-confidence have a ___________ outlook:
   a. Negative b. Arrogant
   c. Outward d. Positive
3. A circular reference is
   a. Geometric modeling tool b. A cell that points to a drawing object
   c. A formula that either directly or indirectly depends on itself
   d. Always erroneous
4. Which of following is Not one of Excel's what-if function?
   a. Goal seek b. Solver
   c. Scenario manager d. Auto Outline
5. When you delete a text box object from a slide in PowerPoint Presentation
   a. The object is deleted but text box and the text inside is left on the slide

b. The text box is deleted and the text is pasted on the slide
c. The text box and text both are deleted
d. None of above

6. Which of the following font effect is not available in PowerPoint Font dialog box?
a. Underline b. Shadow
c. Emboss d. Strikethrough

7. ____________ and ____________ are two parts of email address.
a. Portal address and email address b. User name and domain name
c. Portal address and domain name d. Email address and user name

8. The maximum length of tweet is:
a. 120 words b. No limit
c. 140 words d. 280 words

9. Excel files have a default extension of
a. Xls b. Xlw
c. Wk1 d. 123

10. CPM stands for
a. Character per match b. Correct per match
c. Character per minute d. Correct per minute

Section B: Very Short Questions (2 marks each)

1. Define Slide sorter view?
2. Name the broad categories of biotic components.
3. What is the purpose of the Scroll action of the mouse?

   Or

   What can be represented using Pie chart?
4. Define Toolbar. Name its types.
5. Give advantages to DOS.
6. Explain the characteristics of entrepreneurship.
7. How to type capital letters in a document?
8. Define slide layout in brief?

Section C: Short Questions (3 marks each)

1. Give the steps of copying and moving slides?
2. What is Edubuntu? Give its various features.
3. Write a short note on the Numeric keyboard.

4. Give various factors influencing self-confidence.
5. Explain Mail merge in detail.
6. Give various phases of entrepreneurship development.

Section D: Long Questions (5 marks each)

1. What is a word processor? Give its various features in detail.
2. Give various actions performed using Mouse?

ANSWERS

Section A

1. b	2. d	3. c	4. d	5. c
6. d	7. b	8. d	9. a	10. c

Section B

1. In slide sorter view, the user will get the miniature view of all the slides that are mainly helpful in rearranging, deleting, changing the order of slides, adding translation, setting the timings for the slide show and adding a new slide, and more.
2. The three broad categories of biotic components are: Decomposer, Consumers and Producers.
3. The scroll wheel or wheel mouse is a rubber or plastic wheel located between the left and right buttons. In various applications, there are scrollbars on the right side of the screen in case of having more page length than the screen or monitor length. The scroll wheel on the mouse is used to scroll the page up or down.

   Or

   Pie chart represents the distribution or proportion of each data item over total value. It is most effective to use a pie chart in plotting no more than three categories of data. It depicts data as a series of slices. It is used to portray different items percentage of a store.
4. Toolbar appears below the menu bar. The toolbar, also called the standard toolbar, is a row of boxes, often at the top of an application window, that control various functions of the software.

   In Word processor, there are two types of toolbar:

   a. Standards toolbar

   b. Floating toolbar
5. The following are the advantages of DOS:
   a. We have direct access to the BIOS and its underlying hardware.
   b. Due to its size, it will boot much faster than any windows version; thus, it will run in a smaller system.

  c. It is very lightweight, so it does not have the overhead of the multitasking operating system.
  d. It is good for making workarounds for managing/administering an MS system, and for combining programs.

6. The characteristics of entrepreneurship are:
  a. It is a function of innovation
  b. It is a function of leadership
  c. It is an organization building function
  d. It is a function of high achievement
  e. It is concerned with managing, developing and employing the factors of production
7. To type capital letters, we first have to click on the Caps Lock key available on the left side of the keyboard, and we will observe light on its top right side corner that shows it is on. Now whatever key we will press will come in the capital on the computer. To turn it off, again, click on the Caps lock key.
8. In MS PowerPoint, slide layout refers to the design and placement of different elements on a slide. The default slide layout is a title at the top of the slide, and text underneath the title. However, this default can be modified to include alternate text, images, and even video. The slide layout can be considered an overview of the information being presented by the user.

Section C

1. It is very time-consuming to create the same slide again and again. In Impress, there is an option to reuse the existing slide within the presentation or in any other presentation. To move the slide to another location or to reuse it, use the cut and paste and copy and paste process, respectively.

   To cut and paste or move the slide, perform the following steps:
   - Select the slide, right-click on the mouse button, and select the Cut option from the context menu:
   - Now mark the place in the presentation where you want to move the slide, right-click the mouse button, and select the Paste option from the context menu.

   To copy and paste or reuse the slide, perform the following steps:
   - Select the slide, right-click on the mouse button, and select the Copy option from the context menu.
   - Now mark the place in the presentation where you want to reuse the slide, right-click the mouse button, and select the Paste option from the context menu
2. It has a Graphical User Interface (GUI) that is known as Unity that allows users to interact with the computer system using graphical icons. It allows accessing our data on the web or our computer in a faster way. Earlier its name was Ubuntu Education Edition as it is built on the Ubuntu base. It is one of the best available free software that is designed for homes and computers.

   The following are the features of Edubuntu:
   a. It is compatible with the existing operating systems on the computer machines and happily coexists with them and can share files with these operating systems.

b. Due to the lack of specialized IT staff, educational institutions find it better to use Edubuntu because it enjoys Unix-like security from malware and viruses.

c. A single server can manage multiple computer systems using Edubuntu, making it easily manageable. Edubuntu often helps in reducing the amount of time you spend administering our computers.

d. Edubuntu is free of cost, and therefore it does not add pressure on budgets of educational institutions while providing all the technologies.

e. The main feature is the support provided by communities and experts can be contacted directly via mailing lists and IRC channels, including the Edubuntu developers themselves.

3. Sometimes the numeric keypad is a separate device but not built into a keyboard. This keyboard is usually connected to a computer with either a USB cable or serial connector. This keypad is used when we have to enter massive numeric data. This is the same as a simple calculator that is now also available on the right-hand side of the computer keyboard. It contains the numbers 0 through 9, Decimal point (.), Addition (+), Subtraction (-), Multiplication (*), Division (/) along, Num lock and Enter key.

   Frequently these keys serve as cursor control keys that decide the mode of the numeric keypad. It can also word on dual-mode in one mode; it represents numbers, and on another mode, it acts as various keys like page up, page down, Home, End, and more.

4. There are various factors influencing self-confidence:

   a. **Social factors:** Society that consists of school, friends, family and neighbourhood plays an important role in building and shaping our self-confidence. A long lasting impact is left on our outlook and attitude towards ourselves. How one perceives themselves, gets affected by evaluation from teachers, friends, schoolmates, parents, etc.

   b. **Cultural factors:** Culture or characteristics of a community, society or group is reflected in its beliefs and practices. It includes culture behaviour and development and children growing up in different cultures receive specific inputs from their environment.

   c. **Physical factors:** In development of self-confidence in people an important role is played by healthy mind, healthy physique and good appearance. Person's self-confidence gets affected by the way they appear, in every culture. Behavior, body language and way of speaking reflect the level of confidence.

5. The mail merge feature is used for creating a series of the same documents and sending it to multiple addresses. With this feature, we can merge the main document that can be certificates or letters with a mailing address of various persons. Its name is mal merge because this main document is merged with a mailing address that helps in sending letters, invitations, common documents or certificates for a number of people.

   For example, if we are a manager and want to inform our customers of a meeting, then the meeting purpose is the same in all the documents, but there are changes in the recipient's information such as their first name, last name, and many more.

   In such cases, the mail merge feature saves time and resources. One of the ways is creating a letter in Writer and copy the address from the address list for changing the address or first and last name of each employee. This procedure of copying and changing the name of the employee is very time consuming and tedious. This approach is good when we have to send the letter to a limited number of the person, but it is not possible in case of hundreds or thousands of addresses. In those cases, the use of a mail merge feature is proving to be efficient through this task can be accomplished in one stroke.

Let the common contents be the main document that we want to send to all of our employees or students, and others will be the data source that holds the address list of all employees or students. The actual information is kept in form letter along with the variable names that will be different in every document.

6. There are three phases of entrepreneurship development.
   a. Pre-training or initial phase includes all the activities and preparation required to launch the training program. It involves designing course curriculum for training or selection and identification of potential entrepreneurs and providing initial motivation to them.
   b. Training or development phase of potential entrepreneurs covers special inputs such as business opportunity guidance, technical and managerial inputs, behavioral inputs, and more. In this stage trainers have to judge how far trainees have moved in their entrepreneurial pursuits.
   c. In the Post-training or follow-up phase, the main objective of an entrepreneurship development program is to prepare the participants to start their enterprise. Its success can be judged from the achieved objectives, that is, by getting training how many participants have started their own enterprise.

Section D

1. A word processor is software or a device that allows users to create, edit, and print documents. It enables you to write, store, display text on a screen, modify it by entering commands and characters from the keyboard, and prints it.

   Various basic features of word processor are:

Feature	Explanation
Formatting	Italic, Font name, Boldface, WordArt, Font Color, etc. are some of the formatting features.
Graphic	Charts, drawing, pictures can be added in your documents. This results in overall document presentation enhancement.
Ease and Speed	For text typing a faster and easier method is provided by word processor
Printing	Printout of documents can be easily taken, and a printed version of document can be seen in word processor.
Storage	All documents can be stored for future use.
Mail merge	Through this feature a piece of text can be sent to multiple addresses. Example: Mail merge feature will change the invited guest names, address and send the same document to multiple guests. This results in time and effort saving

Vocabulary and Spell Check	Spell check feature in word processor that keeps your documents free from errors. There is Vocabulary feature of synonyms that gives multiple alternate to same word.

2. Some common actions of the mouse are:
   - **Click or left click:** As mentioned above, the left click of the mouse is used to select an item. To do it, simply press the left button with your index finger.
   - **Double click:** A double click on element or file will open, or it displays a dialog for editing its properties. Sometimes double click is also used to start some program or application.
   - **Right-click:** The right-click anywhere in the interface will display a context sensitive menu or displays a set of commands and available options. The contents of a context menu depend on the position of the cursor when you click. To do it takes the mouse of the desired position then press the right button with your middle finger.
   - **Scroll:** The scroll wheel or wheel mouse is a rubber or plastic wheel located between the left and right buttons. In various applications, there are scrollbars on the right side of the screen in case of having more page length than the screen or monitor length. The scroll wheel on the mouse is used to scroll the page up or down.
   - **Drag and drop:** The drag and drop using the mouse will help in selecting then moving the item or document from one location to another without using cut and paste feature. To do it, simply take the mouse of the desired position, hold down the item by pressing the left side mouse, then drag the object and move the mouse to the desired location and drop the release the left button of the mouse.

INFORMATION TECHNOLOGY (402)

Solved Sample Paper – 4

M.M. 50 **Time: 2 hrs**

General Instructions:

i. Read the question paper carefully.

ii. Question Paper is divided into four sections.

Attempt any of 10 questions from this section:

- **Section A: Multiple choice questions (1 marks each)**

  Attempt any of 6 questions from this section.

- **Section B: Very short Answer (2 marks each)**

  All questions are compulsory in these sections.

- **Section C: Short Answer (3 marks each)**
- **Section D: Long Answer (5 marks each)**

Section A: Multiple Choice Questions (1 marks each)

1. The major pollutant for automobile exhaust is:

   a. NO b. CO

   c. SO_2 d. Soot

2. List Box and Text box:

   a. Are some other than that in a list box the bullets are enabled

   b. Are different. List boxes are used to present lists and can't be created with text boxes

   c. Both a. and b.

   d. None of above

3. How do you magnify your document?

   a. View, Zoom b. Format, Font

   c. Tools, Options d. Tools, Customize

4. There is a __________ number of program buttons available on the top left corner of the title bar.

5. Which of the following is not a primary form of verbal communication?

   a. Oral communication b. Written communication

   c. Body language d. None of these

6. Which of the following colors display the percentage of completion of the lesson?

   a. Red b. Green

   c. Blue d. Yellow

7. Which button do you click to add up a series of numbers?
   a. The autosum button
   b. The Formula button
   c. The quick total button
   d. The total button
8. A small-scale entrepreneur is:
   a. A formal-sector entrepreneur with 11 to 50 employees
   b. A formal-sector entrepreneur with 11 to 49 employees
   c. A formal-sector entrepreneur with 16 to 49 employees
   d. A formal-sector entrepreneur with 16 to 50 employees
9. Out of the given options, which one is not an application area of IT?
   a. Education
   b. Health
   c. Banking
   d. None
10. Excel files have a default extension of:
    a. Xls
    b. Xlw
    c. Wk1
    d. 123

Section B: Very Short Questions (2 marks each)

1. What does WordPad mean?
2. Discuss the Title bar in the PowerPoint Window.
3. Explain the term accountability.

   Or

   What is Oral communication?
4. What do you mean by active cell?
5. Explain Radio as an ICT tool.
6. What does undo do?
7. Name the various input devices of computers.
8. Discuss precedence in terms of performing various operations.

Section C: Short Questions (3 marks each)

1. What is a spreadsheet? Name various existing popular spreadsheet software. Explain in detail about MS Excel along with the steps to start it.
2. Give the six key points on which the green economy is based?
3. What is Ribbon in Microsoft office 2020? Explain its parts.
4. Write a note on selecting a slide layout.
5. Discuss LINUX. Name the features of LINUX.
6. Why should one encrypt data?

Section D: Long Questions (5 marks each)

1. Give formulas of various commonly used basic functions with example.
2. Define workspace view. Give various types of view in detail.

ANSWERS

Section A

1. b	2. a	3. a	4. 3	5. c
6. c	7. a	8. b	9. d	10. a

Section B

1. WordPad is a basic word processor available in every version of Microsoft's operating systems since Windows 95. It can be used to create and modify documents. Although slower to load than Notepad, it can handle graphics and rich formatting, unlike notepad, along with handling larger files. WordPad is well preferred for taking quick notes and text-based writing.
2. On top and middle of the PowerPoint Window, there is a title bar. Both the name of the program and its currently used presentation is displayed on it. The default name of the presentation is Untitled1, and the name of the application is MS PowerPoint.
3. Both accountability and responsibility are similar but have different meanings. As one can share responsibility but accountability is specific to oneself. In case of responsibility one can blame others for any wrong actions but in accountability only we will be responsible and have to answer for our actions.

   Or

   Oral communication is the way of expressing ideas and information through spoken words and considered as a more natural form of communication as compared to written form due to immediate clarification and feedback is involved in it.
4. A thick black color boundary appears on the cell when we click on it that makes it different from non-active cells. Users can enter or edit data only in inactive cells. The name given to this highlighted box is the cell pointer.
5. It is the oldest machine that comes under ICT tool that is used to work as a cricket transmission device, music listening, new device, and more. It is also used in today's era, like in cars; it comes as a built-in part so that one can listen to the news, cricket commentary, Songs, and some of the fun done by RJs.
6. Undo is a function performed to reverse the action of an earlier action. For example, the undo function can undo deleted text in a Word Processor. Some software programs may also have the capability of performing multiple undos.
7. There are various input devices of computers such as: Mouse, Mic, Keyboard, Joystick, Touchscreen, Scanner, and many more, that are used for giving input to the computer.

8. Precedence, in Excel operators, is the rule that specifies the order in which certain operations need to be performed in an expression. For a given expression containing more than two operators, it determines which operations should be calculated first.

Section C

1. A Spreadsheet or worksheet is a file made of numerical data. What makes a spreadsheet software program unique is its ability to calculate values using mathematical cells.

   Microsoft Excel, LibreOffice Calc, Google sheets, Lotus 1-2-3, and Apache OpenOffice Calc are some of the existing popular spreadsheet software.

   The steps need to follow for launching the spreadsheet program is:

   Click on Start > Click on All Programs > Microsoft Office > Microsoft Excel 2010.

   Or

   Choose Start > Type Excel in search programs and files box > Click on the application to start it.

   In some systems we will see the shortcut key of Excel on the desktop. The Excel can start by clicking on the shortcut key.

   Alternatively, search MS Excel by clicking on Show Applications.

2. Green economy is based on the following points:

   a. Clean Transportation
   b. Efficient and cleaner energy production
   c. Water management
   d. Land Management
   e. Greener Buildings
   f. Waste management and disposal

3. Microsoft Office 2010 displays commands in a series of icons, stored on different atbs. The Ribbon makes everything nicely centralised and easy to find, The Ribbob is an expanded toolbar across the top of the page, which is used to create and format a document, It brings the most popular commands to the front. The Ribbon is divided into three sections.

   Tabs: They are designed to be more tasks oriented. Tabs are quite similar to the drop-down menu and clicking on it displays the related groups of commands.

   Groups: Each tab has several groups that show the related commands.

   Commands: A command is a button, clicking on which a certain action could be performed.

4. In the case of the blank presentation, there is a title slide as the first slide, and for the rest of the created slides, there will be title and content in the default layout. The default layout of the slide can be changed by clicking on the layout command given in the slides menu. From this display, the list user can select the desired layout.

   To select a Slide layout, perform the following steps:

   - Select Slide | Slide Layout | Title slide option.

   We can select any of the layouts. For example, we have selected the Layout: Title and 2 Content, and it will be applicable on the right side of the window. Alternatively, we can also select the layout from the Layouts section given on the right side of the presentation.

   Now to further add text to slide, simply click on click add text in the text frame and type the text.

5. Linux OS is an open and free source that was developed by Linus Torvalds in 1991 at AT & T's Bell Laboratories. The main function of Linux OS is to manage the system resources or hardware

and can act as an interface between user and computer system just like other OS. It was designed by considering UNIX compatibility; that's why its functioning is similar to UNIX.

Some of the features of LINUX are: Portable, Open source, Multi-user, Multiprogramming, Hierarchical file system, Shell, Security and Application support.

6. You should encrypt all your data in order to prevent it from unauthorised access. Nowadays many tools are available in windows 7 for encryption of data. These encryption methods and tools are transparent to the user. In very sophisticated systems, unauthorised access may result in physical destruction of the hardware itself.

Section D

1. In MS Excel there are predefined formulas or functions that can be used to perform the required calculations. In the above method where we type formulas to perform the various calculations there will be more chances of error. Arguments 0[0are accepted by it and in return it will give values. Arguments and Structure are two parts that make a complete function.

   The input values to function are known as arguments that can be a text, numbers, logical values, formulas or range of a cell written in between the parenthesis.

   On other hand the basic skeleton is defined by the structure part that makes the basis of writing a general function or its syntax. The syntax is:

   =FUNCTION NAME (argument1, argument2, ……)

   SUM( ): Just like + sign in basic formulas a SUM() function will add all the numbers given in the arguments between the parenthesis of the sum function. Basic steps need to perform are:

   Click on the cell where you want to enter the result > Type =SUM(B2:B6) or =SUM(B2,B6).

   These both functions will give you the sum of data in cell B2 to B6. Users can also enter the direct value in parenthesis instead of entering the cell name. For example =SUM(2,4,6)

   AVERAGE( ): The arithmetic mean and average of the arguments is returned by AVERAGE function. In arguments users can enter the range of cells, direct numbers, both numbers and cell reference. For example:

   - AVERAGE(B2:B6)
   - AVERAGE(B2,B6)

   MAX( ): The MAX function will return the largest value from specified arguments in parenthesis of MAX function. It accepts only numeric data and logical values as arguments and returns zero 0 in other cases. Steps to find the largest value from range of value is:

   - Open the document > Enter the required data > Type =MAX(starting range: Ending range).

   This will return the largest value from the range given in MAX parenthesis.

   COUNT( ): The COUNT function counts the number of cells within the range of cells.

   - For example: COUNT(B2:B6)

     TODAY( ): The current date of a particular cell can be displayed using the function TODAY().
   - Example type =TODAY() function in cell E3 it will display the date of E3 cell.

2. In MS PowerPoint, we can view a presentation with different views like Normal, Slide Sorter, Notes Page and Slide show. The default view of PowerPoint 2010 is Normal view. Various view

options are given in the bottom right side that can be changed by simply clicking on the desired option or you can also select it from the Presentation view group of View tab. This session will give brief details about various types of views available in PowerPoint 2010.

Normal View: This is the default type of view and in this view images, text, animation, video and audio can be added on slide. Users can see the Slide pane, Notes pane and left pane that have Outline and Slide tab. The outline structure of the presentation can easily be viewed in the outline tab and in this text can be easily edited. To open Normal view of presentation performs the following steps:

Click on the Normal view icon present on the bottom right side in the status bar.

Or

Click on View tab > Select Normal view command from Presentation views group.

These both ways will open a Normal view of presentation.

In this view a large view of the current slide appears in the center section of the PowerPoint window. In this section users can enter text, image, animation, graphics, charts, text boxes, hyperlinks, audio and video. Here users can also easily add, arrange or delete slides. The Notes pane is present at the bottom of the MS PowerPoint screen. The space to write speaker notes or information about a particular slide in the presentation is provided by it that can be helpful for the speaker at the time of giving a presentation.

Slide Sorter View: In Slide sorter view users will get the miniature view of all the slides that is mainly helpful in rearranging, deleting, changing order of slides, adding translation, setting the timings for the slide show and adding a new slide, etc. To select the Slide sorter view perform the following steps:

Click on the Slide Sorter view button given in the right bottom side of the status bar next to the Normal view button.

Or

Click on View Tab > Select Slide Sorter view command given in the Presentation views group.

Slide Show View: This view is used to give a presentation to another person. By clicking on this view a presentation will start either from the first or current slide one after another in a defined sequence. The entire screen is occupied by a single slide that helps in seeing how your animation, movies, timings graphics and transition effects look in the actual show. The steps need to follow to select the Slide show view are:

Click on the Slide show view button present in the bottom right side of Status bar.

Or

User F5 key to view the slide show.

Notes Page view: This will give the Note page for a particular slide to edit the speaker notes information which is not visible to other people while giving a presentation. This will help speakers in remembering the important points to discuss and giving to the audience.

Reading View: It is similar to slide show view as in both slides is shown in full screen mode. The only difference in reading view is that title bar and status bar is displayed in it. This view helps in easily navigating during slide show as in slide show view along with that it provides an easy access to window task bar to switch to other open windows or programs.

INFORMATION TECHNOLOGY (402)

Solved Sample Paper – 5

M.M. 50 **Time: 2 hrs**

General Instructions:

i. Read the question paper carefully.

ii. Question Paper is divided into four sections.

Attempt any of 10 questions from this section:

- **Section A: Multiple choice questions (1 marks each)**

  Attempt any of 6 questions from this section.

- **Section B: Very short Answer (2 marks each)**

  All questions are compulsory in these sections.

- **Section C: Short Answer (3 marks each)**
- **Section D: Long Answer (5 marks each)**

Section A: Multiple Choice Questions (1 marks each)

1. The typing errors, slowdown and speed for each chapter is display under ____________ tab?

   a. Next step b. Rating Pane

   c. Detailed statistics d. Error overview

2. In MS-Word, for what does ruler help?

   a. To set tabs b. To set indents

   c. To change page margins d. All of the above

3. Energy that is trapped in the form of organic matter is called:

   a. Conventional energy b. Renewable energy

   c. Biomass energy d. Bioenergy

4. Environmental barriers are the same as ____________ noise.

   a. Physiological b. Psychological

   c. Physical d. Sociological

5. Excel probably considers the cell entry January 1, 2000 to be a

   a. Label b. Value

   c. Formula d. Text string

6. What finger do you use for the letter "b"?

   a. Left pointer b. Right pointer

   c. Left thumb d. Right thumb

7. Transactions can be done anytime, anywhere through the Internet by ___________.
8. Self-management skills do not involve:
   a. Manage emotions
   b. Manage inanimate objects
   c. Manage situations
   d. None of these
9. What is the name of the feature that will allow you to take a step backward if you've made a mistake?
   a. Redo
   b. Cancel
   c. Undo
   d. Backspace
10. In order to edit a chart, you can:
    a. Triple click the chart object
    b. Click and drag the chart object
    c. Double click the chart object
    d. Click the chart object

Section B: Very Short Questions (2 marks each)

1. Define subscript and superscript.
2. Explain the Human-made environment.
3. What are the benefits of Keyboarding skills?

   Or

   Give the precedence of operators in MS Excel?
4. What is the operation of Horizontal scroll bar and Vertical scroll bar?
5. What is indicated by Blue wavy line?
6. What is the objective of the initial phase of Entrepreneurship development?
7. What do you mean by Joint stock company?
8. What is the correct sitting posture to avoid health problems?

Section C: Short Questions (3 marks each)

1. What is PowerPoint? Write down the steps to start PowerPoint in various window software?
2. What do you mean by desktop operating system? Give the features of DOS as well?
3. Give formulas for various typing measurements of speed?
4. Give the characteristics of accountability?
5. What do you mean by formatting text? Give various options for formatting a text in Word processor?
6. Give the role of entrepreneurship in economic development?

Section D: Long Questions (5 marks each)

1. Give in detail about various components of rapid typing software?
2. Name and explain the purpose of various parts of the PowerPoint window?

ANSWERS

Section A

1. c	2. d	3. c	4. c	5. b
6. a	7. E-Banking	8. b	9. c	10. c

Section B

1. After selecting subscript, whatever user type will come below the baseline, and it will look smaller than other normal text in the document.
   - To perform subscript: Select the text and select the Format | Text | Subscriptoption. Or press Shift + Ctrl + B.

   On the other hand, the superscript will place the text above the baseline.
   - To perform subscript: Select the text and select the Format | Text | Superscript option. Or press Shift + Ctrl + P.
2. Human beings interact with the environment and modify it according to their needs. Early humans adapted themselves to the natural surroundings, led a simple life, and fulfilled their requirements from the nature around them.
3. Keyboarding skills are very important in that:
   - They can impact a person's ability to communicate with others in the future, both in social and professional realms.
   - The practice improves the speed of typing, and by it, one can achieve a speed of 60 WPM or even higher.
   - The rate of speed not necessary to be the same for everyone.

Or

3. The precedence of operators in MS Excel is as given below:
   - First: ( )
   - Second: ^
   - Third: /, *
   - Fourth: +, -
4. **Horizontal Scroll bar:** The horizontal bar helps in navigating from left to right, and it is present in the bottom above the status bar.

   Vertical Scroll bar: The vertical bar is present in the right and used to navigate the document from top to bottom.
5. The blue line will come under the word or sentence if there are grammatical errors in the text. These types of errors can be removed by right-clicking on it and selecting the right option. In the context menu that comes after right-clicking on the blue wavy line, the first entry gives the name of suspected grammatical error, and in the second entry, it gives suggestions for correction.

6. Its objective is to provide information and knowledge about entrepreneurship, role of it and available facilities regarding establishment of enterprise to prospective entrepreneurs.
7. It forms a business organization as a voluntary association of persons to carry on business. It normally gives legal status and is subjected to certain legal regulations or association of persons who are contributing money for a common purpose.
8. To avoid any back pain and other problems, sit straight, slightly bending our neck forward while operating the computer keyboard. In ideal typing posture, our keyboard is below our elbow height when seated, with our wrists straight and not planted on the surface of the desk, touching both the feet to the floor.

Section C

1. PowerPoint is a Microsoft presentation program that creates a slideshow of important information, charts, and images to display during a presentation. It is most often used for business and school presentations.

   To start or launch PowerPoint perform the following steps:

   Click on Start > All Programs > Microsoft Office > Microsoft PowerPoint 2010.

   Or

   Choose Start > Type PowerPoint in search programs and files box > Click on the application to start it Or simply double click on PowerPoint icon if it is present on the desktop as a shortcut.

   When we done with any of the above given steps a blank presentation with name Presentation1 will appears on the screen.
2. Disk Operating System (DOS) is a type of system software that runs from a hard disk drive. This also refers to the specific family of DOS, which is known as a Microsoft disk operating system (MS-DOS). An operating system is anything that controls and commands the hardware of the computer and its peripheral device's control over the program and its functionality.

   The following are the features of DOS:

   a. The mouse cannot be used to operate it, Input in it is through basic system commands. It is a free OS.

   b. It uses a text-based interface and requires text and codes to operate.

   c. It does not support a graphical interface.

   d. It is a single-user operating system.

   e. It is a character-based interface system. It provides a command-line interface that allows users to type commands on DOS Prompt.

   f. It supports independent device input and output processes, or in another word, it can be said that it has the ability to function on a wide variety of devices regardless of the used software and hardware.

   g. It is programmed in assembly language that converts commands to binary language. Its speed is very high as compared to other operating systems.

3. Formulas for various typing measurements of speed are:
   - CPM = (Characters without errors + Characters with errors) / Time spent in minutes
   - Net CPM = CPM - (Characters with errors / Time spent in minutes)
   - KPM = (Keystrokes without errors + Keystrokes with errors) / Time spent in minutes
   - Net KPM = KPM - (Keystrokes with errors / Time spent in minutes)
   - WPM = (Words without errors + Words with errors) / Time spent in minutes
   - Net WPM = WPM - (Words with errors / Time spent in minutes)
4. Some of the characteristics of accountability are:
   a. **Avoid procrastination:** Procrastination means avoiding the important tasks that need to be completed. This includes choosing an easy task rather than doing the important difficult task. This must be avoided.
   b. Adopting a problem solving attitude is required in every area of work. Sometimes people have to face difficult situations even after planning or prioritizing everything. In these cases, a problem solving attitude helps in achieving goals on time.
   c. **Managing your own emotions:** As emotions prevent us from working towards best and constructive solutions.
   d. **Coping with distress:** There can be situations of injuries, accidents, illness, and death in a family that may impact our physical and emotional well-being. In those situations, surround ourself with people who can provide us the required practical and emotional support.
5. The formatting text means the formatting of paragraphs and characters. In case you want to format the particular text in the document, select the text you want to format nd apply the required text formatting features.

In the Word processor, there are a number of options for formatting text that can be chosen according to suitability. Various methods of formatting text are:

a. Using the menu options from the menu bar.
b. Using the readily available buttons on the formatting toolbar.
c. Using the context menu by right-clicking on the selecting text.
d. Using a keyboard shortcut.

Some of them are:

a. **Change of font-size:** You can change the font size by selecting font size.
   - **Change of font style:** You can change the font style by either making it bold, italic, or underline.
   - **Change of font type:** You can change the font type by selecting font dropdown.
   - **Change of font color:** You can change the font color by selecting the font color icon.

   To apply any of the effects, firstly select the text, then press the desired buttons given on the formatting toolbar.

   Changing text case: You can change the case of the text. In Word processor Writer, there are 6 change case options. There are six options of text case in Word processor that can be applied to text by selecting

6. The entrepreneur is the key to create new enterprises that energize the economy and rejuvenate the established enterprises that make up the economic structure. In the economic system an important role is played by entrepreneurship and nature and scope of it is determined by the economic system.

   The entrepreneur or entrepreneurship initiate and sustain the process of economic development in the following ways:

   a. Capital information
   b. Generation of employment
   c. Improve per capital income
   d. Improve living standard
   e. Balanced regional development
   f. Improve economy of country
   g. Improve living standards of people

Section D

1. There are various components of RapidTyping software as given below:

   a. **Title bar:** It consists of program modes, option buttons, and three control buttons.
   b. The Option buttons are available on the top right corner of the Title bar that helps in changing the background, themes, help, logout, sound, text color, font, and more.
   c. There are three program buttons available on the top left corner of the title bar. Click on the current lesson button given in the very first position from left to check the current lesson. Click on student statics next to the current lesson button gives the current statics of the students typing. The last one is the Lesson editor that is used to edit the lesson settings.
   d. On the extreme right side, there are three control buttons Minimize, Maximize and Close that are used to reduce the size of RapidTyping window, maximize the size, and to close the window, respectively.
   e. **Toolbar:** Current course and current lesson control come under this section that helps the user to select the current course from the above-given list Introduction, beginner, experienced, advanced and testing modes. On the other hand, current lesson control consists of going back to the beginning, pause/resume current lesson, checking accuracy, elapsed lesson time, and current speed.
   f. **Text Area:** Text area or text panel is an area where the user sees the text typed by them.
   g. **Status bar:** This bar is present on the bottom of the text area that consists of tips, progress bar, and volume control. The length of the lesson, metronome to help a user to know about the lesson details, comes under the progress bar.
   h. **Virtual keyboard:** This is the keyboard of RapidTyping software that helps the user to learn touch typing with all our fingers.

2. Various parts of PowerPoint main window are:

   Title Bar: On top and middle of the word window there is a title bar. Both the name of the program and its currently used presentation is displayed on it. The default name of presentation is Presentation1 and name of application is Microsoft PowerPoint.

   Quick access toolbar: It is located in the top left side of the title bar. The frequently used common buttons are present on it. Redo, Undo and save are three buttons that are present by default on it. We can remove or add other button through the drop down arrow present on it.

   Ribbon: On clicking of any tab a ribbon appears. It contains tab, groups and commands. On top of ribbon button there are 9 tabs that contains groups of related commands. All related commands are organized in groups. The name of Tabs are File, Home, Insert, Design, Translations, Animations, Slide Show, Review and View. By default the home tab appears after launching the word.

   Window Management Buttons: In PowerPoint there are Minimizer, Maximize or restore and Close window management buttons. Each have their own functioning as to hide buttons from desktop screen a minimize button is used and to enlarge window back to its standard size a maximize button is used and to close application a Close button is used.

   Slides Pane: The thumbnail of slides is display in slides pane or a place where user can design the slides. It allow user to add new slides, remove or rearrange slides.

   Slides: On slide user can add text, image, video and audio.

   Outline Tab: It displays the outline of text present in each slide and in this view user can directly edit their text.

   Status Bar: In the bottom of PowerPoint window there is status bar that gives working document status like slide number, Name of theme, Spell check, View and Zoom slider options. View button consists of Normal view, Slide sorter view, Reading view and Slide show view and the zoom slider in right side helps to zoom in and out the slide.

   Notes Pane: Users can type the personal notes about the current slide in notes pane and these notes do not appear on the screen in slide show mode.

   Splitter Bar: The size of panes can be adjusted using these two horizontal and vertical bars.

   Layouts: In Impress you can also prepare ypu own layput and safe it for future use.

   Status Bar: In the bottom of Impress window there is status bar that gives working presentation status like slide number, Name of theme, Spell check, View and Zoom slider options. You can turned off the status bar in the View menu by selecting the Status bar command.

   Custom Animation: In a slide there are various animation features for drawings, text, etc., through which you can add, change or remove animation features.

   Zoom Control: It help in changing the scale of the text and pictures in the document for view. It does not affect the physical document.

   Insertion Point: It is a location of the blinking cursor where your text will appear as you type anything.

INFORMATION TECHNOLOGY (402)

Solved Sample Paper – 6

M.M. 50 **Time: 2 hrs**

General Instructions:

i. Read the question paper carefully.

ii. Question Paper is divided into four sections.

Attempt any of 10 questions from this section:

- **Section A: Multiple choice questions (1 marks each)**
  Attempt any of 6 questions from this section.
- **Section B: Very short Answer (2 marks each)**
  All questions are compulsory in these sections.
- **Section C: Short Answer (3 marks each)**
- **Section D: Long Answer (5 marks each)**

Section A: Multiple Choice Questions (1 marks each)

1. Password, Date, Time settings of BIOS are stored in ____________.
   a. Internal memory b. CMOS chip
   c. External memory d. Booting process
2. The home row keys are asdf jkio.
   a. True b. False
3. Which would you choose to list Synonyms & Antonyms of a selected word?
   a. Tools, Spelling & Grammar b. Tools, Language
   c. Tools, Options d. Insert, Cross-reference
4. Hyperlinks can be:
   a. Text b. Drawing objects
   c. Pictures d. All of above
5. Which of the following font effects is not available in PowerPoint Font dialog box?
   a. Underline b. Shadow
   c. Emboss d. Strikethrough
6. What is the full form of 3Rs to conserve natural resources?
   a. Reduce, Reuse and Remove b. Reduce, Remove and Recycle
   c. Reduce, Reuse and Recycle d. Reduce, Reuse and Repair

7. To begin typing a new line of text, press:
   a. The SPACE key b. The BACKSPACE key
   c. The ENTER key d. The ESCAPE key
8. The header and footer command are located on the __________ tab.
   a. Home b. Insert
   c. View d. Header
9. Which of the following is not a type of phrase?
   a. Noun b. Adjective
   c. Adverbial d. Pronoun
10. To remove the line that you just typed you would use the __________ key.
   a. Enter b. Delete
   c. Backspace d. Tab

Section B: Very Short Questions (2 marks each)

1. Define Normal view of the workspace.
2. What do you mean by Ecosystem?
3. What do you mean by sentence?
4. Give the operation of the mouse?
5. What is the purpose of using MAX function in Excel? Write down the steps to use it.
6. Define slide layout in brief.
7. Give examples of service as business activity?
8. What is the purpose of the drag and drop action of a mouse?

Section C: Short Questions (3 marks each)

1. What do you mean by Business? Give various types of business.
2. Give in brief the three primary components of all ecosystems.
3. What do you mean by Typing accuracy? Give various formulas for typing accuracy?
4. Write a note on positioning of fingers on the keyboard.
5. Write a note on creating a document in Word.
6. What do you mean by organization skills of self-management? Explain the SMART strategy used in it.

1. Name and give brief about various typing measurements of speed rates. Give formulas for various typing measurements of speed.
2. Give various characteristics of good quality preparation in detail?

Section D: Long Questions (5 marks each)

1. Name and give brief about various typing measurements of speed rates. Give formulas for various typing measurements of speed.
2. Give various characteristics of good quality preparation in detail?

ANSWERS

Section A

1. b	2. b	3. b	4. d	5. d
6. c	7. c	8. b	9. d	10. c

Section B

1. This is the default type of view, and in this view, images, text, animation, video, and audio can be added on the slide. This is also the main view for working with individual slides and format or design. In this view, the position of the slide will be in the middle, and on the left side, there is a slide pane.
2. An ecosystem can be defined as a functional unit of nature in which living organisms interact with each other and also with the surrounding physical environment. Ecosystems can be as small as ponds or as large as sea or forest.
3. A group of words that make complete sense is called a sentence. It must consist of predicate and subject.

   Examples:

   Not a sentence: Understand too much is there.

   Sentence: There is too much to understand.
4. All mouse have their own mechanism operation according to their types, but all of them accomplish the same task. In some of the mice, there is a light beam at the bottom of the mouse that tracks the motion or mouse on the other hand, some use a tracking ball for the same purpose. For performing the same job on laptops, there is either a very short stick or small flat surface.
5. The MAX function will return the largest value from specified arguments in parenthesis of MAX function. It accepts only numeric data and logical values as arguments and returns zero 0 in other cases. Steps to find the largest value from a range of value is:
   - Open the document and enter the required data. Type =MAX(starting range: Ending range).
   - This will return the largest value from the range given in MAX parenthesis.
6. In MS PowerPoint, slide layout refers to the design and placement of different elements on a slide. The default slide layout is a title at the top of the slide, and text underneath the title. However, this default can be modified to include alternate text, images, and even video. The slide layout can be considered an overview of the information being presented by the user.

7. This includes service given below:
    - Lawyers
    - Chartered accountant
    - Salons
    - Sports academic
    - Hotels
8. The drag and drop using the mouse will help in selecting then moving the item or document from one location to another without using cut and paste feature. To do it, simply take the mouse of the desired position, hold down the item by pressing the left side mouse, then drag the object and move the mouse to the desired location and drop the release on the left button of the mouse.

Section C

1. Business is an organization or economic system where goods and services are exchanged for one another or for money.

   Various types of business are classified into four types are:

    a. Service is a business that provides products with no physical form. These companies or firms provide expertise, professional skills, advice and other similar services. It involves the execution of specialized personal services on the basis of training, education and knowledge.

    b. Manufacturing is concerned with the transformation and manufacturing of raw materials, labor, and other production processes to manufacture goods. To make new products raw materials are bought by manufacturers.

    c. Merchandising is also known as trading or buy and sell business. In this, merchandise business firms buy products at wholesale prices and further sell it at retail prices to other customers or retailers.

    d. Hybrid is a company that is classified into more than one type of business or it is a mixed type of business.
2. The three primary components of all ecosystems are:

    a. **Autotrophs:** Autotrophs are producers of energy and majority of autotrophs in an ecosystem are made by plants as they convert energy from sun or other sources into food.

    b. **Heterotrophs:** Heterotrophs are the consumers of energy and these organisms directly or indirectly depend upon the autotrophs of their food. They are also known as consumers and most of the heterotrophs are animals.

    c. **Non-living matter:** It is leaf litter, soil, sediments and other organic matter found on ground or at the bottom of an aquatic system.
3. It defined as the percentage of correct entries out of total entries typed. Different formulas for typing accuracy calculation are:
    - Accuracy in words = (100% - Words with errors* 100%)/Total number of Words
    - Accuracy in characters = (100% - Characters with errors* 100%)/Total number of characters
    - Accuracy in keystrokes = (100% - Incorrect keystrokes * 100%)/Total number of keystrokes

4. Nowadays pen and pencil work have been replaced with a computer keyboard. The correct positioning of fingers comes with mastery typewriting skills or attaining the necessary knowledge and skill of keyboard.

   a. During the keyboard operation in Home Row or Horizontal approach, all the eight fingers of both the hands rest on Home keys F, D, S, A, and J, K, L.

   b. Left-hand fingers must be placed on F, D, S, A, and right-hand fingers on J, K, L. As from these keys the user is able to reach all other keys easily.

   c. Fingers should be kept on correct keys and keep hands and fingers near to base position.

   In-home row approach fingers are trained to make the correct movement to the other keys, and it returns immediately to its home key after it has depressed the corresponding key in any other row. The thumb of both hands is kept at the Spacebar to enter space between the words. While using uppercase letters and symbols, type them using one hand, and use another hand to Shift key. To press the Enter key, use the little finger of the right hand.

5. The creation of documents is almost the same for all operating systems. Various steps to create a document are:

   Click on File Menu given on the top of the window. Click on New Document:

   a. Type whatever you want to type in the created text document.

   b. After writing the required text in it, the next step is to save the file. To save a file, click on the File | Save option. This will open a new Save As window, give the name of the file and select the required file format from Save As type drop-down.

   c. After giving a name to the file and selecting the required format type, click on the Save button given in the right bottom side of Save As window.

6. In organization skill-management, we can plan your time, energy and resources effectively when we are organized in work and life. Being organized will help us save our energy and time and help in completing tasks effectively and get more productive results. The most important thing we should know is what should be done first and what can be done later. This is called prioritization of tasks.

   Breaking down goals into smaller and fruitful tasks: To achieve a bigger task or goal, we need to divide it into smaller parts and define our targets using SMART strategy. In SMART strategy, S stands for specific, M stands for Measurable (like divide your tasks whose completion gives measurable outcome), A stands for Achievable (that means set a task that can be achieved), R stands for Realistic, and T stands for Time bound.

Section D

1. Various typing measurements of speed rates:

   a. **CPM:** CPM stands for characters per minute that are used to view the character per minute speed progress.

   b. **Net CPM:** Net CPM is the CPM without characters with errors.

   c. **KPS:** KPS stands for Keystroke per second.

d. **CPS:** CPS stands for characters per second that are used to view the character per second speed progress.

e. **KPM:** KPM stands for keystrokes per minute, and it defines the number of keystrokes in a one minute period of time.

f. **Net KPM:** It is the KPM without keystrokes with errors.

g. **WPS:** WPS stands for words per second that are used to view the word per second speed progress.

h. **WPM:** WPM stands for Word per minute that is used to view the word per minute speed progress.

Formulas for various typing measurements of speed are:

a. CPM = (Characters without errors + Characters with errors) / Time spent in minutes

b. Net CPM = CPM - (Characters with errors / Time spent in minutes)

c. KPM = (Keystrokes without errors + Keystrokes with errors) / Time spent in minutes

d. Net KPM = KPM - (Keystrokes with errors / Time spent in minutes)

e. WPM = (Words without errors + Words with errors) / Time spent in minutes

f. Net WPM = WPM - (Words with errors / Time spent in minutes)

2. Various points or characteristics of good presentation are:
   - **Opening and closing phrases:** The opening and closing of the presentation must be carefully framed by keeping in view the situation, subject, and audience. The opening should attract a listener's attention and their interest using some relevant statements related to your subject.
   - **Number of lines:** Try to limit the number of lines; it should be between 5 to 8 lines in one slide. As adding a paragraph or more number of lines takes more time to read a single slide due to the use of small font sizes to add more data.
   - **Font size:** The font size of the text on presentation is also one of the important things to be considered. Font size is set according to the distance between the screen and the audience.
   - **Use of quotations:** The speaker should be very cautious in using quotations. He should avoid the use of a large number of quotations as well as long.
   - **Correctly use grammar and language:** The use of language and grammar in the presentation should be correct because the mistakes in it will replicate the number of persons in the audience.
   - **Insert images, clips, tables, or graphs:** Use images, clips, tables, or graphs in the presentation to make it more attractive to the audience.
   - **Simplicity:** The speaker must deliver the speech in simple words and sentences as it makes speech more effective.
   - **Use colors:** Try to use dark colors, bold letters with different fonts for highlighting certain points. For fonts, try to use fair or silent background and dark colors.
   - **Animation, sounds, and videos:** Make sure you don't insert or include more than one animation or video in one slide as it will overlap the sounds and can also result in confusion to the audience.
   - **Availability of voice and words:** The very first requirement of good presentation in any given circumstance, the voice and words should be audible.

INFORMATION TECHNOLOGY (402)

Solved Sample Paper – 7

M.M. 50 **Time: 2 hrs**

General Instructions:

i. Read the question paper carefully.

ii. Question Paper is divided into four sections.

Attempt any of 10 questions from this section:

- **Section A: Multiple choice questions (1 marks each)**
  Attempt any of 6 questions from this section.
- **Section B: Very short Answer (2 marks each)**
  All questions are compulsory in these sections.
- **Section C: Short Answer (3 marks each)**
- **Section D: Long Answer (5 marks each)**

Section A: Multiple Choice Questions (1 marks each)

1. ____________ refers to the failure to acknowledge or recognize the limits of personal knowledge, skills and experience.
2. All worksheet formula:
   a. Manipulate values b. Manipulate labels
   c. Return a formula result d. Use the addition operator
3. WPS stands for
   a. Weight per strokes b. Words per strokes
   c. Weight per second d. Words per second
4. CPS in typing measurement of speed rats gives character written per second. (True/False)
5. Bold, Italic, Regular are known as
   a. font styles b. font effects
   c. word art d. text effects
6. Which of the following statement is false?
   a. If you choose to select from one of the pre-made slide layouts, you can change the positioning
   b. If you choose to select from the pre-made slide layouts, you cannot delete the objects in the layout.
   c. Blank Slide is at the top of the 'Content Layouts' area in the Slide Layout panel.
   d. All of above are false statements

7. ROM is a ___________ memory.
   a. Volatile
   b. Primary
   c. non-volatile
   d. Secondary
8. The fingertips of your right hand should always be placed on these keys:
   a. J, k, l, semicolon
   b. U, I, o, p
   c. K, I, semicolon, apostrophe
   d. H, j, k, semicolon
9. Ctrl + U:
   a. Undelete the previously deleted text
   b. Undo the last changes
   c. Underline the document name
   d. Underline the selected text
10. What is the full form of EEG?
    a. Electricagram
    b. Electroencepalogy
    c. Electroencephalography
    d. Electrocardiogram

Section B: Very Short Questions (2 marks each)

1. What is the difference between Delete and backspace button in terms of operation?
2. What is environment?
3. What is Rapid Touch Tutor?

   Or

   What is Absolute referencing?
4. Define Non-printing character.
5. What do you mean by Multi User OS?
6. What are the rewards of entrepreneurship?
7. What is the purpose of using the MAX function in Excel? Write down the steps to use it.
8. Give examples of manufacturing business activity.

Section C: Short Questions (3 marks each)

1. Define Presentation. Give various elements of presentation.
2. Write a complete step of starting a computer.
3. Give various courses provided by it.
4. Give in detail the three key skills of self-management.
5. Give the usage of any 7 keys of a computer keyboard?
6. Explain the types of business enterprises in your country.

Section D: Long Questions (5 marks each)

1. Explain selecting criteria of consecutive or non-consecutive text in a Word processor?
2. Discuss Typing ergonomics? Give various typing ergonomics.

ANSWERS

Section A

1. Overconfidence		2. c	3. d	4. True	
5. a	6. b	7. c	8. a	9. d	10. c

Section B

1. There is a difference in the Delete and Backspace button. As the delete button will delete the content from the right of the corner, on the other hand, the Backspace key or button will delete from the left of the corner. Pressing any of the Delete or Backspace keys will delete one character at a time.
2. Environment is a sum of the total of the elements, factors and conditions in the surroundings which may have an impact on the development, action or survival of an organism or group of organisms.
3. Rapid Typing Tutor is a free and open-source software that is designed for learning typing skills on the computer. Learning to type with a rapid typing tutor is a fun and typing game. To use a computer more efficiently by kids and adults, a rapid touch typing tutor is used.

   Or

   There are cases when we don't want a cell reference to change when copied to other cells, as happens in relative referencing. In those cases, absolute referencing is used as it will not change when copied and filled in another cell. In case of absolute referencing, a $ symbol is used before the column name and row number that make it constant for any formula.
4. A non-printing character, also called a control character, is a number that represents a non-written or non-printable character (letter, number, or symbol). Some control characters represent audible or silent signals to be sent or received. Other control characters (ASCII code) include the backspace, line feed, form feed, carriage return, escape, and delete.
5. It allows us to use more than one user to use the same computer at the same time. Unix, Linux, Microsoft window 2000, and many more are some of the multi-user OS. Windows 2000 was the first version of Windows that allowed creating multiple user accounts on a single machine.
6. Various rewards of entrepreneurship are:
   - Being the boss
   - Freedom to do anything
   - Be creative

- Building an enterprise
- Own schedule
- Business from home
- Excitement

7. The MAX function will return the largest value from specified arguments in parenthesis of MAX function. It accepts only numeric data and logical values as arguments and returns zero 0 in other cases. Steps to find the largest value from a range of value is:
   a. Open the document and enter the required data. Type =MAX(starting range: Ending range).
   b. This will return the largest value from the range given in MAX parenthesis.
8. Examples of manufacturing business activity are to make steel, iron ore is used as a raw material. Yarn and wool are used as raw materials in cotton and wool/textile companies. Electronic parts, LCD screens, and batteries are used as raw materials by mobile phone manufacturing companies.

Section C

1. Presentation software is used to display information in a sequence of slides or slide shows that is used in colleges, schools, organizations, and many more, for various purposes.

   Various elements of presentation are:

   a. **Be prepared:** Being prepared is one of the most important elements of the presentation. This depends on how many times we practice our speed that must be 30 hours of rehearsal time for every hour we will be speaking.
   b. **Give of yourself:** While giving the presentation try to use personal examples, but make sure it supports our point and message we want to convey through the presentation.
   c. **Stay relaxed:** We will be relaxed if we have prepared for our presentation. Also, focus on our message instead of an audience and use gestures like walking patterns, and many more.
   d. **It has a clear objective:** Define our goals clearly, right at the outside. The objective of our presentation will drive everything from our script to our slide deck.
   e. **It's useful to our audience:** Make sure our presentation should genuinely and meaningfully offer value to its audience. That means sharing key strategies that have worked for us, offering up enlightening data or insights, or telling a story that may be able to learn from.
   f. **Use little text in your presentation desk:** Don't give the audience a reading assignment. As it will make the overall experience of our presentation less enjoyable. Our audience is liable to feel distracted and even a little stressed.
2. To start a computer: Switch on the main power supply | Switches on the UPS and monitor.
   a. By starting it, the booting process begins to check all the hardware and software installed in the computer is working properly and load all the needed files.
   b. The next step is a booting process that checks the functionality of all the connected hardware that includes primary and secondary storage devices.
   c. Once the computer passes the booting process the next step is checking a Complementary Metal Oxide Semiconductor (CMOS) chip that stores the settings like password, date, and time of Basic Input Output System (BIOS).

d. The BIOS includes instructions for loading basic computer hardware, and its main motive is to boot up an operating system on the computer.

e. The operating system is loaded on the RAM after completion of all the steps of BIOS, then to define user configurations, a pre-configuration start-up routine is executed by OS.

f. Then with our username and password, we can log in to the computer system, and the operating system desktop will appear if we have entered the correct credentials. In some systems, we will not find the option of entering a username and password if we have not set it.

3. According to the level of difficulty, various courses are provided by Rapid typing are:
   - Introduction: It covers all the characters typed on a keyboard
   - Beginner course: It helps in knowing the positions of various keys like uppercase, lowercase, and special characters on a keyboard and helps in knowing the keys without looking at the keyboard.
   - **Experience course:** The frequently used words and syllabus are memorized, and improve the speed of typing comes under this.
   - **Advanced skills:** The user learns to type the actual text that comes with an improvement in typing skills.
   - **Testing:** There are advanced typing tests in the testing part of the course that helps in knowing the accuracy and typing speed of the user.

4. The three key skills of self-management are:
   - **Initiative:** It is the ability to work without always getting instructions for what needs to be done. This requires people to believe in their own capabilities even in difficult situations. It means using your mind and driving yourself to achieve your goals. Self belief is must in initiative as then only you will be able to go out of your way to solve problems without the need to be instructed by others.
   - **Organization:** You can plan your time, energy and resources effectively when you are organized in work and life. Being organized will help us save our energy and time and help in completing tasks effectively and get more productive results. The most important thing we should know is what should be done first and what can be done later. This is called prioritization of tasks.
   - **Accountability:** Both accountability and responsibility are similar but have different meanings. As one can share responsibility but accountability is specific to oneself. In case of responsibility one can blame others for any wrong actions but in accountability only you will be responsible and have to answer for your actions. If you say to yourself that you are accountable then it means you take ownership of responsibilities that come to your way.

5. There are 104 keys of keyboard. Out of which functioning of seven keys of keyboard are:
   - **Alphabetic keys:** There are 26 alphabets keys on the keyboard from A to Z. But these keys are not present in the alphabetic order. You can use these keys for typing words, sentences, or paragraphs.

- **Alt key:** Alt key stands for Alternate that is press together with another ley so that the other key does something different from what it usually does. It is like a second control key.
- **Arrow keys:** There are four arrow keys for moving the cursor up, down, left, or right, and these are used for moving the cursor in the respective direction.
- **Backspace key:** Backspace key is similar to the delete key that removes texts in a word. It deletes the text in the left of the cursor and moves the cursor to that position.
- **Caps lock key:** It is a toggle key, on pressing it every alphabetic character will be in uppercase.
- **Ctrl key:** The Ctrl key stands for the control key that is used in combination with other keys for doing a particular operation. It is the keyboard shortcut key.
- **Delete key:** It deletes or removes the characters at the current position of the cursor or also the selected object or text. The difference between backspace and delete is that the backspace key will delete the text and move the cursor; on the other hand, by deleting a text, the cursor will not move. Sometimes this key is simply referred to as Del.
- **Enter key or Return key:** It is used to makes the computer perform an action or start a new line of writing, or it move the cursor to the beginning of the next line.
- **Esc key:** The Esc key in the computer stands for the Escape key that is used to send special codes to devices and exit from the programs and tasks and return to a previous menu.
- **Function keys:** It is a special button on a keyboard that is used for a particular operation in a program. The special keys on the computer keyboard are labeled as F1 to F12.

6. Various types of business enterprises in our country are:
   a. Joint stock company forms a business organization as a voluntary association of persons to carry on business. It normally gives legal status and is subjected to certain legal regulations or association of persons who are contributing money for a common purpose. The board of directors handles the management of such companies.
   b. Cooperative society is a society whose purpose is to render services to its members and to the public. It is democratically operated and controlled on a non-profit basis as their basic motive is to meet social, economic and cultural needs of its members.
   c. Sole proprietorship business is owned by a single person who provides the entire capital, bears all the risks and independently manages it. This form is mainly adopted for small scale independent businesses, thus it is also known as one man business organization.
   d. Partnership is another form of non-cooperative form of enterprise. In this more than one person carries a lawful business and shares its profits. Even losses are borne equally by themselves. In this form of business, people from similar backgrounds or different skills join together to carry one business and they all are legally responsible for the business.

Section D

1. To perform the operation of copy and paste or cut and paste operation, we have to select the text that will be highlighted after selection. Firstly text is selected before editing the text. As we can do editing part of the selected text.

Selection criteria: There are various ways of selecting the text according to the part of the text we want to select. In general, to select the text, we just have to swipe the mouse cursor over the text. Various tricks of selection for increasing speed are:

Technique	Action
Single Word	Double click on single word
Sentence	Triple click
Paragraph	Click four times in a row
Multiple selection	Press Ctrl key while clicking
Continuous selection	Click at the beginning then press Shift key and swipe the mouse till the end then again click at the end
All text	Ctrl +A

Selecting Non-consecutive text items: Sometimes there can be cases in which we have to select a part of the text from a paragraph instead of continuous text. In Word processor, we can either use keyboard or mouse to select the non-consecutive text.

a. **By using Keyboard:** To select a non-consecutive text item using keyboard, perform the following steps:

   Select the starting text > Press Ctrl and select the required text, column or block by pressing right arrow key, This puts writer in 'Adding selection mode' > Use arrow keys to move to the start of the next piece of text to be selected > Press Shift key and select the next piece of text.

   Repeat it to select all the required text then press Esc key to exit the mode and come back to basic mode.

b. By using Mouse: To select a non-consecutive text item using mouse, perform the following steps:

   Select the starting text > Hold down or press Ctrl key and move the mouse to select the next piece of text.

   Repeat it to select all the required text.

2. Typing ergonomics is used to reduce the stress, strain, and wear and tear of our joints as we repeatedly type away. This also helps in maintaining effective typewriting, along with maintaining accuracy and speed. Some of the factors that come under typing ergonomics are given below:

   Sitting posture: To avoid any back pain and other problems, sit straight, slightly bending our neck forward while operating the computer keyboard. In ideal typing posture, our keyboard is below our elbow height when seated, with our wrists straight and not planted on the surface of the desk, touching both the feet to the floor. The key positions to achieve the most ergonomic and comfortable typing position are:

   i. **Position of feet:** Keep our both the feet flat on the floor, and we can also use a footstool if required.

ii. **Placement of mouse and keyboard:** Our mouse and keyboard should be near to each other around in the distance of 20 cms that helps in operating the keyboard smoothly and effortlessly. The keyboard should be flat on the desk or sloping gently away from us.

iii. **Placement of monitor:** Do not bend our neck while working on the monitor as bending forward will create too much pressure on our discs. Keep our upper border of the screen at eye level or slightly below it, and its distance depends on the screen size. If our screen is of 17 inches, then keep an approximate distance of 50 to 80 cms.

iv. **Placement of chair and table:** The height of the chair and table should be chosen so as to expose the shoulder, wrist, and arm muscles to the least possible strain. The wrist can touch the tabletop in front of the keyboard. Keep keyboards and printers like vibrating devices on separate tables. From the floor, the height of the under-desk keyboard drawer or tabletop must be 68 to 73 cm. Make sure there is enough space in the table for our legs.

iv. **Placement of matter to be typed:** The writing matter must be kept either to the left side or right side of the keyboard or on anything that has a sloping surface.

INFORMATION TECHNOLOGY (402)

Solved Sample Paper – 8

M.M. 50 **Time: 2 hrs**

General Instructions:

i. Read the question paper carefully.

ii. Question Paper is divided into four sections.

Attempt any of 10 questions from this section:

- **Section A: Multiple choice questions (1 marks each)**
  Attempt any of 6 questions from this section.
- **Section B: Very short Answer (2 marks each)**
  All questions are compulsory in these sections.
- **Section C: Short Answer (3 marks each)**
- **Section D: Long Answer (5 marks each)**

Section A: Multiple Choice Questions (1 marks each)

1. Green economy is essential for ___________ sustainability and future prosperity.
   a. Human b. Animal
   c. Life d. Resource
2. In the slide layout panel how many layouts are available for text layout by default?
   a. 4 b. 7
   c. 12 d. None of above
3. Which of the following can you change using the page setup dialog box?
   a. Margins b. Page orientation
   c. Vertical alignment d. All of the above
4. Sender sends a message and in response gets ___________ from the receiver.
   a. Nothing b. Result
   c. Feedback d. All of these
5. How do you delete a column?
   a. Select the column heading you want to delete and select the Delete Row button on the standard toolbar
   b. Select the column heading you want to delete and select Insert Delete from the menu

c. Select the row heading you want to delete and select Edit>Delete from the menu
d. Right click the column heading you want to delete and select delete from the shortcut menu

6. There is ____________ keyboard in RapidTyping.
   a. 2 keyboard　　b. Fictional keyboard
   c. Virtual keyboard　　d. Best keyboard
7. The shortcut keys for the ____________ character formatting is ctrl shift+ plus sign.
   a. Case of letters　　b. Underline words, not spaces
   c. Superscript　　d. All capital letters
8. R in SMART strategy stands for ____________.
   a. Real　　b. Rate
   c. Realistic　　d. Required
9. Which of the following organizations gratify only the needs of their parent company and do not serve external clients?
   a. Multinational Companies　　b. Indian Service Providers
   c. Global In-house Centers　　d. All of these
10. ____________ displays the percentage and number of characters, words, spaces, and specific characters in the lesson.
   a. Editing panel　　b. Table analysis text
   c. Virtual keyboard　　d. Lesson plan

Section B: Very Short Questions (2 marks each)

1. Write down the full form of SMART strategy.

   OR

   Define the allocation of keys to fingers on the fourth or number row.
2. Define Aligning paragraph?
3. Name common text formatting features in MS Word.
4. What is the short form of closing PowerPoint?
5. Define BPO services.
6. Explain Floating Toolbar.
7. Name the Home row keys.
8. What can be represented using Pie chart?

Section C: Short Questions (3 marks each)

1. Define selecting criteria of consecutive text in document of Word processor?
2. Give various processes of the workplace where IT is used.

3. Write a note on formatting a range of cell to be seen as labels.
4. Write a short note on creating a Header and footer and page number?
5. Is it possible to insert a duplicate slide in PowerPoint? If Yes, then write down the steps to insert a duplicate slide in it.
6. What is Mixed Referencing?

Section D: Long Questions (5 marks each)

1. Write down the steps to use a mail merge?
2. How to group and ungroup the objects in Slide?

ANSWERS

Section A

1. d	2. a	3. d	4. c	5. d
6. c	7. c	8. c	9. c	10. b

Section B

1. In SMART Strategy, S stands for specific, M stands for Measurable like divide your tasks whose completion gives measurable outcome, A stands for Achievable that means set a task that can be achieved, R stands for Realistic, T stands for Time bound.

   OR

   To operate or press a key on the fourth or number row, you have to use a little finger to type 1, ring finger to type 2 and middle finger to type 3 and 4 and 5 number is press using index or forefinger. Similarly, the little finger of the right hand is used to press 0, ring finger to type 9, and 8 number is press using middle fingers of right hand and index or forefingers are used to press number 7 and 6.
2. The position of paragraph between the page margins is known as paragraph alignment. By default, the text is aligned on the left side of the document, and the right margins in the document are known as horizontal text alignment.
3. The common Text formatting features in MS Word are:
   a. **Change of Font size:** We can change the font size by selecting font size.
   b. **Change of Font Style:** We can change the font style by either making it bold, italic or underline.
   c. **Change of Font type:** We can change the font type by selecting font drop down.
   d. **Change of Font colour:** We can change the font colour by selecting font colour icon.
4. The short form of closing PowerPoint is: Press Alt +F4 or Press Ctrl + Q keys of keyboard.
5. BPO is the abbreviation of Business Process Outsourcing services that are meant to perform business operations through an outside service provider. In the BPO, complete transfer of the business process or the function to an external service provider takes place.

6. The floating toolbar is just below the Standard Toolbar. It is context sensitive that shows the tools relevant to the current position of the cursor or the selected object.
7. The home keys are the row of keys on the computer keyboard we fingers rest on when not typing. The Alphabets ASDF are home keys for left hand and LKJ along with semicolon ";" are for right hand. For both hands the thumb rest on the spacebar.
8. Pie chart represents the distribution or proportion of each data item over total value. It is most effective to use a pie chart in plotting no more than three categories of data. It depicts data as a series of slices. It is used to portray different items percentage of a store.

Section C

1. To perform the operation of copy and paste or cut and paste operation, you have to select the text that will be highlighted after selection. Firstly text is selected before editing the text. As you can do editing part of the selected text.

   Selection criteria: There are various ways of selecting the text according to the part of the text you want to select. In general, to select the text, you just have to swipe the mouse cursor over the text. Various tricks of selection for increasing speed are:

Technique	Action
Single Word	Double click on single word
Sentence	Triple click
Paragraph	Click four times in a row
Multiple selection	Press Ctrl key while clicking
Continuous selection	Click at the beginning then press Shift key and swipe the mouse1 till the end then again click at the end
All text	Ctrl +A

2. Technology is such an integral part of a 21-st century workplace that any business without some level of technical knowledge will fail. In workplaces or offices, computers and its applications are used to perform work more effectively that makes computer use as prevalent. Some offices or companies may find functioning without them is virtually impossible.
3. There are some cases in which there is a need to format a range of cells to be seen as labels. These cases can come in telephone numbers in which every country STD code starts with 0. But when you enter the telephone number in a spreadsheet with prefix as 0, then the "0" will disappears from the telephone number because, in a spreadsheet, it stores as a numeric value that does not have a preceding 0 or zero.

   But to take 0 as a prefix in the spreadsheet, we take numeric values as text. To format the selected range of cells that consist ofa telephone number as text, perform the following steps:

   - Select the range of cells and click on the Format tab menu bar. Click on the cell, and Format Cells dialog box will open
   - Click on Numbers tab and select Text and click OK button
   - Now you can enter the numbers in a spreadsheet with prefix 0.

4. In a multi-page document, or for creating a file, book, there is a need for adding header and footer to document.

   The header is a top section of the document that includes text or graphics. They usually contain important information like company name, department name, school name, college name, logo, page numbers, document title, author name, and many more. To insert a header in the document, select the Insert tab from the top of the writer window. Click on **Header and Footer | Header** option.

   Footer is a bottom section of the documents that contain a special area and special text. Footer contains almost the same elements as header like document name, college name, school name, date, page number, title, phone number, and more. To insert a header in the document, select the Insert tab from the top of the writer window. Click on **Header and Footer | Footer** option.

5. Yes, You can insert a duplicate slide in PowerPoint.

   To insert a duplicate slide, perform the following steps and using the options given below:

   Select the slide from Slide Pane > Select Slide menu bar > Duplicate Slide.

   OR

   Another option is: Right click on the slide > Select Duplicate Slide from the menu.

6. Mixed is the combination of relative and absolute referencing. It is used when we have to make some row number and column name constant and some has to vary accordingly. To make the row number and column name constant a $ sign is used before it.

   For example: We have entered the number of class 9th students in English, =hindi, maths and IT subjects. In Total marks we have taken the sum in which the relative referencing is used as arguments cell name is varying according to their position. Same is for average but in GR total column we can observe that the Sum column is varying and grace marks column name is constant and $ sign is added before the row number. This shows the mixed referencing.

Section D

1. Corresponding values are kept in the data source that is a set of a mailing address in multiple rows and columns that is also known as a database. In this, each row contains the record of each person that has other fields such as name, address, roll no., and many more. The best way to create a database is the use of spreadsheets as table format is used in this for storing the data. Another option is the use of mail wizard for creating an address book during a mail merge.

   Steps to use mail merge are: Create a new document, and add data to be sent to multiple people, to create a new document, perform the following steps:

   1. Click on Tool tab as shown in the following screenshot.
   2. Choose the Mail Merge Wizard option, and a new window will appear.
   3. Select Starting document from Mail Merge Wizard dialog box and choose to Use the current document option. Click on the Next button given at the bottom of the dialog box.
   4. Then, click on the document type and choose the E-mail message. Click on Next button.
   5. Click on address list, and Select Address List window will open that contains an option for creating the recipient list.

6. In the above window, click on Select Address List, and a Select Address List dialog box will open.
7. In the above-given dialog box, click on Add... to add various members' addresses. Click on Create... button, this will open a New Address List window will open.
8. If you want to customize the fields of recipient information. Click on Customise...button and Customise Address List window will appear
9. Now click on Add... button, delete or rename any of the fields. In this, you can also change the order of appearance of the fields using the up/down arrow button given on the Customise Address List window.
10. The Add... option is used for creating a new field, Delete... is used to delete an unnecessary field, and Rename... is used to change the name of the field.
11. Then click on OK button to close the list, and this will open a Save As dialog box.
12. In Save As dialog box, add the name in File name text box and click on Save if you want to save the document in the opened location; otherwise, Change the location and Save it.
13. A list window will appear after saving the list that will display the entire recipient list created by you.
14. From the list you can select any of the created lists and click on OK button to send the mail to the selected list
15. After selecting the address from the list, the next step is to click on Create Salutation and add the required information, and then click on Next button
16. In the next step, a Writer will display the document with Mail Merge Toolbar

2 Grouping Objects: There are some cases in which you have to use various shapes to create flowchart, figure, etc. In those cases you can draw various shapes then group all the objects to a single object. Now instead of formatting it individually, you can format it as a single object, move, rotate, delete, etc.

To select more than one object, perform the following steps:

- Select all objects by pressing Ctrl or Shift key

  OR

  Ctrl + A

  To group the selected object, perform the following steps:
- Select Format > Group

  OR
- Right click on any object > Select Group option from context menu

  OR
- Ctrl + Shift + G keys

Ungrouping Objects: There are some cases in which you have to insert any new object in grouped objects. In those cases there is option of ungroup objects in Impress. To ungroup the objects, perform the following steps:

- Select the group > Right click on it > Select Ungroup option from context menu

  OR

  Ctrl + Alt + Shift + G keys

INFORMATION TECHNOLOGY (402)

Solved Sample Paper – 9

M.M. 50 **Time: 2 hrs**

General Instructions:

i. Read the question paper carefully.

ii. Question Paper is divided into four sections.

Attempt any of 10 questions from this section:

- **Section A: Multiple choice questions (1 marks each)**
  Attempt any of 6 questions from this section.
- **Section B: Very short Answer (2 marks each)**
  All questions are compulsory in these sections.
- **Section C: Short Answer (3 marks each)**
- **Section D: Long Answer (5 marks each)**

Section A: Multiple Choice Questions (1 marks each)

1. It is important to prepare a __________ to accommodate the planned tasks and other activities.
   a. Schedule b. Date-sheet
   c. Planning d. Task-sheet
2. MS-Word automatically moves the text to the next line when it reaches the right edge of the screen and is called:
   a. Carriage Return b. Enter
   c. Word Wrap d. None of the above
3. ITeS is an abbreviation of __________.
   a. Information technology end-to-end services
   b. Information tech and end-user services
   c. Information technology-enabled services
   d. Information tech enable services
4. Which of the following is not an example of written communication?
   a. Emails b. Reports
   c. body language d. Letters
5. Hyperlinks can be
   a. Text b. Drawing objects
   c. Pictures d. All of above

6. The fingertips of your left hand should always be placed on these keys:
   a. Q, w, e, r
   b. A, s, d, f
   c. A, d, g, i
   d. A, d, f, g
7. What PowerPoint feature will you use to apply motion effects to different objects of a slide?
   a. Slide Transition
   b. Slide Design
   c. Animation Objects
   d. Animation Scheme
8. Which of the following color display the percentage of completion of the lesson?
   a. Red
   b. Green
   c. Blue
   d. Yellow
9. Our dress code is an example of ___________ communication.
10. What steps should one take to build confidence?
    a. Set goals in life
    b. Appreciate oneself for all the achievements
    c. Always think positively
    d. Talk to people who are confident

Section B: Very Short Questions (2 marks each)

1. Give any two disadvantages of written communication.
2. What do you understand by overexploitation of Natural resources?
3. What is the guide keys?

   OR

   Give the shortcut key of undo and redo the changes?
4. What is the default position of Label in Excel spreadsheet?
5. Explain Encoding and Decoding.
6. What is the use of a Cardiac Screening machine?
7. How to control the size of the view?
8. Define Fill handle in MS office?

Section C: Short Questions (3 marks each)

1. How IT is used in Home computing?
2. Define an EEG machine and what is its purpose?
3. Give the allocation of keys to fingers on the first or lower row?
4. Define Rapid Touch Typing.
5. What is the purpose of the Error window in Rapid Touch Typing?
6. What is subscript and superscript in PowerPoint? How does it affect the data?

Section D: Long Questions (5 marks each)

1. Explain any three view option of PowerPoint.
2. Write down the steps to insert an image from file and gallery? What are the ways to move, resize and rotate the image.

ANSWERS

Section A

1. a	2. c	3. c	4. c	5. d
6. b	7. d	8. c	9. Non-verbal	10. b

Section B

1. The disadvantages of Written communication are:
   a. Written content has legal validity.
   b. It helps user to draft comprehensive message.
   c. In case of lengthy messages it is considered suitable mode.
2. This means overuse of natural resources to such extent that it almost reaches a stage of enervation. We can see this phenomenon in the exploitation of Forest and natural vegetation, Grazing pastures, Medical plants, Wildlife, Fossil fuels, and Fish stock and water aquifers.
3. The guide keys are those keys that help in moving the cursor using the keyboard. On a computer keyboard, the F key for the left hand and J key for the right hand are guide keys. This helps touch typists in placing the fingers correctly on home keys.

   OR

   For undo: Press Ctrl + Z key
   For Redo: Press Ctrl + Y key
4. The default position of MS Excel is Left side.
5. Encoding or converting data or information into the coded language that is not understood by any other person.

   The encoded information is decoded at the receiver side to understand the sent message or information. The messages should be decoded according to the pattern used by the receiver while encoding it that helps in having correct information.
6. The Cardiac Screening Machine is used to display the physiology of the heart and its inside movements. This machine is mainly used for diagnosis of problems related to heart like thinning of veins and then according recommend treatment.
7. To view the presentation in different sizes, there is an option to control the size of the view. You can control the size of the view using the Zoom and View Layout dialog box opens in the View tab. Using it, you can increase zoom or enter your own value that must be a whole number. Or one can use Zoom slider.

8. In MS Excel Fill Handle tool, we can fill the next cell by dragging it with the next predefined value. For example: We want to fill the Roll numbers, Month, Week, Days, etc., then we can input one or two in sequence then select them and drag it to the next cell or till that we want to continue that series of sequence.

Section C

1. The purpose of use of IT in Home computing is for working at homes a personal computer or PC are used for performing household work. It is used for surfing the web, creating and listening to music, playing games, doing household accounts, playing puzzles, etc.

   The aim of personal computers at home is to help families in need to use the internet and develop basic computer skills in their everyday lives that results in an increase in children literacy rate.
2. EEG stands for Electroencephalography Machine that is a test used to evaluate the electrical activity in the brain. Brain cells communicate with each other through electrical impulses. The potential problems associated with this activity can be detected by this machine. It also records and tracks the patterns of brain waves. The small electrical probes are attached to the head for receiving the electrical impulses of the brain and send signals to a computer for recording the results.
3. To operate or press keys on the first row that contains Z, X, C, V, B, N, M, Comma, Full Stop, and / sign. To work on these keys, simply take your pinky finger off to key A and move it up to the below first key Z. Use the middle finger of the left hand to type C key then again take that finger back to home key D. Rest keys are also pressed in the same way by using fingers used for corresponding keys in Home or second row.
4. Rapid Typing Tutor is a free and open source software that is designed for learning typing skills on the computer. Learning typing with Rapid typing tutor is a fun and typing game. To use computers more efficiently by kids and adults a rapid touch-typing tutor is used. There are a number of games, exercises, and training sessions that sharpen the skills of users and help them to work efficiently in a short time.
5. The detailed statistics for the current lesson can be seen on the Error tab that shows our errors and delays percentage both in the table and graphical view. This helps in understanding the hard letters to type for us. We can switch between Errors in percent charts and delays in percent charts. In bar charts the letters used in the lesson are given on the X-axis and delays or errors related to each letter are shown on Y-axis. The chart will not be shown for no errors and delays for a certain character.
6. After selecting subscript whatever user type will come below the baseline and it will look smaller than other normal text in the document.
   - To perform subscript: Select the text > Select the Format > Text > Subscript Or Press Shift + Ctrl + B

   On other hand the superscript will place the text above the baseline.
   - To perform subscript: Select the text > Select the Format > Text > Superscript Or Press Shift + Ctrl + P

Section D

1. In MS PowerPoint we can view a presentation with different views like Normal, Outline, Slide Sorter, Notes, Slide Master, Notes Master and Handout Master. The default view of Impress is Normal view. Various view options can be selected from the View menu.

Normal View: This is the default type of view and in this view images, text, animation, video and audio can be added on slide. This is also a main view for working with individual slides and format or design. In this view, the position of slide will be in middle and on the left side there is slide pane.

To select the Normal view, Click on View Menu bar or tab > Select Normal view command

Outline View: In Outline View of presentation, there are all slides of the presentation in a sequence. In Outline format you can see each slide and in workspace only the text is visible in each slide. It also displays the slide text in the form of a structure.

To select the Outline view, Click on View Menu bar or tab > Select Outline view command

Notes View: In Notes view, there is option to add notes for each slide that contains the information for presenter. This information is not visible to other person while giving presentation. This will help speaker in remembering the important points to discuss and giving to audience.

To select the Notes view, Click on View Menu bar or tab > Select Notes view command

2. To insert an image from the gallery, perform the following steps:

   Select Insert Menu bar > Media > Gallery and the available themes with images are displayed in the gallery.

   Now from gallery you can select the theme and find a suitable from by scrolling > Click on the image > Drag it onto the workspace > Release the mouse button and image will be observe on the slide.

   Formatting Images: We have learnt to insert an image but sometimes there can be requirements of formatting that image such as moving, resizing, rotating, etc. Various formatting on inserted images are:

   Moving Images: To move an inserted image in the slide, perform the following steps:

   Click on Image > wait till the cursor changes to hand shape > Click on image and drag it to the desired position > Release the mouse button.

   Resizing Images: To resize an inserted image in the slide, perform the following steps:

   Click on Image > Put the cursor on one of the selection handles on the image and the cursor will change the shape by giving a graphical representation of the direction of the resizing > Click and drag the image to resize it > Release the mouse button

   Rotating Images: In Impress, you can also rotate the image in any direction using a rotating icon or manually. To rotate an inserted image in the slide, perform the following steps:

   Click on Image > Click on Rotate icon on the Line and Filling toolbar > Click again on the selected image and shape and colour of selection handles get changed > Click the mouse and move it in the required direction > Release the mouse button.

   Formatting using the Image toolbar: Instead of formatting manually, you can also format the image using the Image toolbar. It comes under the properties window after selecting the image in the slide.

   The toolbar contains a number of formatting options. Other option to display Image toolbar is: Select View menu bar > Toolbars > Image

INFORMATION TECHNOLOGY (402)

Solved Sample Paper – 10

M.M. 50 **Time: 2 hrs**

General Instructions:

i. Read the question paper carefully.

ii. Question Paper is divided into four sections.

Attempt any of 10 questions from this section:

- **Section A: Multiple choice questions (1 marks each)**
  Attempt any of 6 questions from this section.
- **Section B: Very short Answer (2 marks each)**
  All questions are compulsory in these sections.
- **Section C: Short Answer (3 marks each)**
- **Section D: Long Answer (5 marks each)**

Section A: Multiple Choice Questions (1 marks each)

1. A character that is raised and smaller above the baseline is known as:
   a. Outlined b. Raised
   c. Superscript d. Subscript
2. ______________ is a study, design, development, implementation, storing, support and management of all computer-based information systems.
   a. Communication b. Information Technology
   c. Process d. Technology
3. Which of the following is not a learning app?
   a. Javatpoint b. Khan Academy
   c. WhatsApp d. Kindle books
4. The CAPS LOCK key is used to capitalize the first letter when you are typing someone's name. (True/False)
5. Multiple calculations can be made in a single formula using:
   a. Standard formulas b. Array formula
   c. Complex formulas d. Smart formula

6. What feature will you use to apply motion effects in between a slide exits and another enters?
   a. Slide Transition
   b. Slide Design
   c. Animation Objects
   d. Animation Scheme
7. Which of the following is the shortcut key to open format cells dialog box?
   a. Ctrl + O
   b. Ctrl + 1
   c. Shift + O
   d. Shift + I
8. Which management function involves measuring results, comparing results to expectations, and taking corrective action?
   a. Planning
   b. Organizing
   c. Leading
   d. Controlling
9. The effects of radioactive pollutants depends upon:
   a. Rate of difficult
   b. Energy releasing capacity
   c. Rate of deposition of the contaminant
   d. All of these
10. The pollution which does not persistent harm to life supporting system is:
    a. Noise pollution
    b. Radiation pollution
    c. Organochlorine pollution
    d. All of these

Section B: Very Short Questions (2 marks each)

1. Define external peripheral devices memory card reader.
2. Give any two advantages and disadvantages of non-verbal communication.
3. What is a worksheet? How can one insert more worksheets?
4. What is the full form of SMART?
5. Define Notepad.
6. What is the operation of NIC cards?
7. Name various methods that can be used to provide training.
8. What do you mean by cell and Cell address in MS Excel sheet?

Section C: Short Questions (3 marks each)

1. Give uses of the Internet.
2. Explain the categorization of the environment.
3. Discuss the various techniques or stages of Touch typing.
4. Write a short note on creating a Header and footer and page number.
5. How to enter data in the worksheet including various types of data one can enter in it?
6. Write a short note on how self-confidence, self-esteem, self-monitoring and SWOT building self-confidence.

Section D: Long Questions (5 marks each)

1. Explain in detail about the allocation of keys to fingers.
2. Discuss the various characteristics of good quality preparation in detail.

ANSWERS

Section A

1. c	2. b	3. c	4. False	5. b
6. a	7. b	8. d	9. d	10. a

Section B

1. Memory card reader enables the read and writing to a memory card and is mostly used to transfer data to a computer or other storing devices. The main function of a card is to quickly transfer files to an SD card and take backup of the most important files.
2. The following are the advantages:
   a. It complements verbal communication.
   b. It helps handicapped people.

   The following are the disadvantages:
   a. Not easy to recognize non-verbal messages that can result in miscommunication.
   b. Necessary explanation and long conversation are not possible.
3. Worksheet is a grid that consists of a number of rows and columns in which data is entered by a user. By default, there is a single worksheet in Excel, named Sheet1displayed at the bottom left side. In the case of working with huge data, further sheets can be added in it by clicking on the insert worksheet button + sign given before the default sheet.
4. In SMART strategy, S stands for specific, M stands for Measurable (like divide your tasks whose completion gives measurable outcome), A stands for Achievable (that means set a task that can be achieved), R stands for Realistic, and T stands for Time bound.
5. Notepad is a generic text editor included with all versions of Microsoft Windows that allows us to create, open, and read plaintext files. If the file contains special formatting or is not a plaintext file, it cannot be read in Microsoft Notepad. The image is a small example of what the Microsoft Notepad may look like while running.
6. Network interface card or NIC is used to connect the computer with the local area network (LAN) and comes in the form of cards that fit in the computer motherboard expansion slot. There is a need for at least one NIC in every computer that is a part of the network, and most of them are designed for a specific type of protocol, media, and network.
7. Various methods that can be used to provide training are through lectures, Written instructions method, Conferences, Practical, Demonstration method and Individual or group training.

8. Cell is an intersection of row and column. Number of cells makes a worksheet. It is the basic element of a spreadsheet. It holds data, such as text, numbers, formulas, and so on. Each row is identified by row number, and column number that is known as the address of the cell.

Section C

1. The Internet has been the most useful technology of modern times that helps us in our daily lives, development of personal and professional lives.
    a. The Internet is used for communication.
    b. Gathering information by users for educational purposes.
    c. It is used by business professionals or doctors to filter the necessary information for their use.
    d. It is used in maintaining contacts with friends and relatives or with clients
    e. It is used for online shopping.
    f. It is used for Entertainment purposes by playing videos on YouTube, or watching serials on Netflix, and more.
    g. The Internet in Office spaces allows having conferences and meetings over the Internet.
    h. It is used for online booking tickets of hotels, movies, trains, planes, and buses.
    - Used for social networking as one can share their interests, stories, and knowledge with their friends and family around the world through Twitter, Facebook, and more.
2. Environment is categorized into two types as given below:
    a. **Natural environment:** It includes living and non-living things like air, animals, water, land and plants. Lithosphere is the solid crust or hard top layer of the earth that is made up of minerals and rocks and covered with a thin layer of soil. It is an irregular surface with plateaus, valleys, plains and mountains.
    The natural environment is subdivided into biotic and abiotic components:
        i. **Biotic components:** Biotic components are living components of an ecosystem. Some of these factors include animals, plants, bacteria, and fungus. On the basis of energy requirement, the source biotic component can be further classified.
        ii. **Abiotic components:** Abiotic components are physical or chemical factors that act on living organisms at any part of their life. Light, soil, air, water, and minerals are forms of abiotic components of an ecosystem.
    b. **Human-made environment:** Human beings interact with the environment and modify it according to their needs. Early humans adapted themselves to the natural surroundings, led a simple life, and fulfilled their requirements from the nature around them.
3. Various benefits of TouchTyping is Increase in speed, accuracy, and more. A touch typist never looks at the keyboard while typing and hits the right keys with practice. This is a fast way of typing as a typist has to only focus on text being typed, reading the words and phrases as the fingers type the text. To learn touch typing, various stages are:
    a. **Stage one:** From this stage process of touch typing starts from where the user learns the home row on the keyboard. In this touch, the typist is restricted from viewing the keyboard while the whole typing focus should be on reading the words, the text being typed. In this user, learn about the lower row, upper rows, number row, uppercase letters, and special symbols.

b. **Stage two:** In this stage, remembering of the frequently used syllabus and typing words containing this syllabus is done.

c. **Stage third:** In this stage, the user will type the actual text with the acquired skills.

4. In a multi-page document, or for creating a file, there is a need for adding header and footer to the document.

   The header is a top section of the document that includes text or graphics. They usually contain important information like company name, department name, school name, college name, logo, page numbers, document title, author name, and many more. To insert a header in the document, select the Insert tab from the top of the writer window. Click on Header and Footer | Header option.
   Footer is a bottom section of the documents that contain a special area and special text. Footer contains almost the same elements as header like document name, college name, school name, date, page number, title, phone number, and more. To insert a header in the document, select the Insert tab from the top of the writer window. Click on Header and Footer | Footer option.

5. In MS Excel, there is a need to select the cell before entering data in the worksheet or cell. To select a cell, simply position the pointer in that particular cell. We can enter a label, values, or formula data in any cell.

   - **Label:** It is any text that can be letters, numbers, and special symbols that entered using the keyboard. By default, labels are aligned on the left side.
   - **Values:** It is the numeric data consisting of only numbers. By defaults, they are aligned on the right side. Various forms of values are integer, decimal, and more.
   - **Formulae:** It is the expression that begins with an equals (=) sign. The formula is always started by= and followed by values, cell addresses, and functions. After entering the formula in a cell, then the value of the equation is displayed in the cell, and the formulas bar contains the formula.
   - **Values:** It is the numeric data consisting of only numbers. By defaults, they are aligned on the right side. Various forms of values are integer, decimal, and more.
   - **Formulae:** It is the expression that begins with an equals (=) sign. The formula is always started by= and followed by values, cell addresses, and functions. After entering the formula in a cell, then the value of the equation is displayed in the cell, and the formulas bar contains the formula.

6. Building self-confidence is the process that takes efforts and commitment and it requires having a positive attitude about yourself. In this self-confidence is the belief in our own ability in dealing with various challenges and events. One can happily or easily tackle difficult situations by having confidence. Be assertive and have faith in your beliefs. Self-esteem is a general feeling about our own self. People with low self-esteem are more affected by others' opinions about them. On other hand people with high self-esteem have positive feelings about themselves. Then self-monitoring is the extent to which we base our behavior on cues from other people and situations. Someone with high self-monitoring pays attention to what behavior is appropriate in certain situations like being hygienic, staying clean, spending time with positive people and

having high ethical standards. And The SWOT stands for Strength, Weakness, Opportunity, and Threat and it is a useful technique for understanding opportunities and challenges. This analysis helps in recognizing one's abilities and talents along with choosing opportunities utilizing their core strengths. This is used for outlining the suitable goals and applies organizing skills on it.

Section D

1. The various allocation of keys to fingers are:
   a. Allocation of keys to fingers on the second or home row: To operate the second row, you have to place your fingers of each hand on the allotted keys. Now you will leave with key g and h that is operated by the forefingers of the left and right hand, respectively.
   b. Allocation of keys to fingers on the first or lower row: To operate or press keys on the first row that contains Z, X, C, V, B, N, M, Comma, Full Stop, and / sign. To work on these keys,simply take your pinky finger off to key A and move it up to the below first key Z. Use the middle finger of the left hand to type C key then again take that finger back to home key D. Rest keys are also pressed in the same way by using fingers used for corresponding keys in IIome or second row.
   c. Allocation of keys to fingers on the third or upper row: To operate or press any key on the third or upper row, you have to take your finger from a to q by little left-hand finger and from (;) top by the little right-hand finger. Then the third finger is placed to the adjoining keys w and o, so on. While typing on the upper row, firstly, keep your fingers on the home row. Now take your left-hand pinky finger off the A key and move it up to the top row first key Q. Use the middle finger of your left hand from D up to E key then again come back to the home key. The left-hand index finger is used to type R then return to the F key. Now lift the fingers of the right hand and strike upper row keys one after another and type p, o, I, u, and y. Make sure that at a time, only one finger should move and keep the rest of the fingers on the home row at their respective position.
   d. Allocation of keys to fingers on the fourth or number row: To operate or press a key on the fourth or number row, you have to use a little finger to type 1, ring finger to type 2 and middle finger to type 3 and 4 and 5 number is pressed using index or forefinger. Similarly, the little finger of the right hand is used to press 0, ring finger to type 9, and 8 number is pressed using middle fingers of right hand and index or forefingers are used to press number 7 and 6.
2. Various points or characteristics of good presentation are:
   a. **Opening and closing phrases:** The opening and closing of the presentation must be carefully framed by keeping in view the situation, subject, and audience. The opening should attract a listener's attention and their interest using some relevant statements related to our subject.
   b. **Number of lines:** Try to limit the number of lines; it should be between 5 to 8 lines in one slide. Adding a paragraph or more number of lines takes more time to read a single slide due to the use of small font sizes to add more data.
   c. **Font size:** The font size of the text on presentation is also one of the important things to be considered. Font size is set according to the distance between the screen and the audience.

  d. **Use of quotations:** The speaker should be very cautious in using quotations. He should avoid the use of a large number of quotations as well as long.
  e. **Correctly use grammar and language:** The use of language and grammar in the presentation should be correct because the mistakes in it will replicate the number of persons in the audience.

f. **Insert images, clips, tables, or graphs:** Use images, clips, tables, or graphs in the presentation to make it more attractive to the audience.

g. **Simplicity:** The speaker must deliver the speech in simple words and sentences as it makes speech more effective.

h. **Use colors:** Try to use dark colors, bold letters with different fonts for highlighting certain points. For fonts, try to use fair or silent background and dark colors.

i. **Animation, sounds, and videos:** Make sure you don't insert or include more than one animation or video in one slide as it will overlap the sounds and can also result in confusion to the audience.

j. **Availability of voice and words:** The very first requirement of good presentation in any given circumstance, the voice and words should be audible.

Self-Assessment

INFORMATION TECHNOLOGY (402)

Self-Assessment Paper – 1

M.M. 50 **Time: 2 hrs**

General Instructions:

i. Read the question paper carefully.

ii. Question Paper is divided into four sections.

Attempt any of 10 questions from this section:

- **Section A: Multiple choice questions (1 marks each)**
  Attempt any of 6 questions from this section.
- **Section B: Very short Answer (2 marks each)**
  All questions are compulsory in these sections.
- **Section C: Short Answer (3 marks each)**
- **Section D: Long Answer (5 marks each)**

Section A: Multiple Choice Questions (1 marks each)

1. ____________ refers to data or instructions fed into a computer.
2. The ____________ pointer is used in graphical based text processing applications.
   a. Grabber pointer b. Selection Pointer
   c. H-Beam d. I-Beam
3. CPM stands for ____________.
4. Which of the following is a benefit of use of IT in business?
   a. Improve efficiency b. Minimise waste
   c. Increase profit d. All of these
5. The range of Columns in Excel?
   a. 1 to 124 b. 1 to 1048576
   c. 1 to 1024 d. 1 to 1023
6. While Touch typing, make use of ____________ fingers.
   a. 4 b. 2
   c. 10 d. 5
7. You can select all text in the document by pressing ____________ keys on the keyboard.
   a. Ctrl + C b. Ctrl + V
   c. Ctrl + A d. Ctrl + X

8. The output of 634.8877777 after selecting two decimal places from Format Cells dialog box will be:
   a. 6.3488 b. 634.8877
   c. 63.488 d. 634.88
9. Which of the following is not a valid document view?
   a. Inline b. Draft
   c. Print Layout d. Web Layout
10. The change in background colour of paragraph comes under ____________ tab.
   a. Page b. Borders
   c. Alignment d. Area

Section B: Very Short Questions (2 marks each)

1. Give full form of any three: MODEM, CPU, ALU, NIC and Wi-Fi.
2. What is Habitat Distinction?
3. What do you mean by Greenhouse Gases?

   OR

   Define EEH machine and what is its purpose?
4. Explain I-beam mouse pointer on the document.
5. What is the purpose of the Redo button in the PowerPoint window?
6. Name various types of Referencing in Excel.
7. How to control the size of the view in presentation?
8. What is the operation of Slide Pane in Presentation?

Section C: Short Questions (3 marks each)

1. Write down the components of a computer network established between the two offices of a company across the cities.
2. Write difference between a text editor and word processor software. Write the name of any text editor or word processor available in the market.
3. Which are the prominent areas where IT is used in science and engineering?
4. Write down the steps to create charts using spreadsheets.
5. How to group and ungroup the objects in Slide?
6. Give various techniques of selecting text.

Section D: Long Questions (5 marks each)

1. Explain the purpose of Grammar and spelling checking utility of MS-Word. How it can be applied or performed in word documents?
2. What is the purpose of conditional formatting in Ms-Excel? Also discuss the purpose of highlight cell rules and Top/Bottom rules.

INFORMATION TECHNOLOGY (402)

Self-Assessment Paper – 2

M.M. 50 **Time: 2 hrs**

General Instructions:

i. Read the question paper carefully.

ii. Question Paper is divided into four sections.

Attempt any of 10 questions from this section:

- **Section A: Multiple choice questions (1 marks each)**
  Attempt any of 6 questions from this section.
- **Section B: Very short Answer (2 marks each)**
  All questions are compulsory in these sections.
- **Section C: Short Answer (3 marks each)**
- **Section D: Long Answer (5 marks each)**

Section A: Multiple Choice Questions (1 marks each)

1. Being accountable means being ____________ for your actions.
2. Which of the following is not a type of sentence?
   a. Subject b. Predicate
   c. Phrase d. Sentence
3. Which of the following activity is related to E-commerce?
   a. Inventory Management b. Online Shopping
   c. Socialising d. Transactions
4. What is the full form of Cc?
   a. Carbon cone b. Copy Cat
   c. Carbon Copy d. Copy Carbon
5. Which of the following is not a pronged approach proposed by UNEP for attaining green economy?
   a. Low Carbon growth b. Low oxygen growth
   c. Resource efficiency d. Social Inclusivity
6. When you send an e-mail, its copy is automatically stored in the ____________ folder.

7. Number keypad help to enter:
   a. Number b. Special symbols
   c. Letters d. All of these
8. In __________ area of Touch typing you see the text typed by you.
   a. Error window b. Letters panel
   c. Panel d. Text panel
9. __________ is used to change a physical object into its digital version.
   a. Printer b. Scanner
   c. Light Pen d. All of these
10. The cell is identified by __________
    a. A column letter b. A row letter
    c. A column letter followed by row letter
    d. All of these

Section B: Very Short Questions (2 marks each)

1. How positive thinking helps in achieving self-confidence.
2. What do you understand by Guide Keys? Name the Guide keys of a
   (a) computer keyboard
   (b) typewriter
3. What is an MRI machine?
   Or
   What are the sources of pollution?
4. Is it possible to remove the new addition in the document using a single command? If, yes then name that command.
   (**Hint:** There is command in left side of Title bar that is used for performing that operation, You can also use the shortcut keys for the same)
5. Which are the different areas of healthcare in which IT is used?
6. Solve it: Cell A1 contains the number 10 and B1 contains 5. What will be the contents of cell C1, if the formula =A1+B1*2^3 is entered in cell C1?
7. How to control the size of the view in presentation?
8. Which feature of Animations tab is useful for adding sound to slide transition?

Section C: Short Questions (3 marks each)

1. What is the functioning of a computer and its three main units with the help of a block diagram?
2. Use both the methods of inserting the table in the document. Write a short note on both methods.
3. Why is low carbon growth the chief aim of green economy? How do the increased carbon emissions impact the environment?
4. Why do you apply Wrap Text formatting on cells? Write down the steps to perform it.
5. Define Blog in brief?
6. How one can insert lesson into Rapid Typing Software from external file?

Section D: Long Questions (5 marks each)

1. What is the purpose of insert utility of MS-Excel? Highlight the different types of graph which we can inserted in excel
2. What is the purpose of different border styles of table in MS-Word? Also differentiate between the draw tables and insert table functionality.

INFORMATION TECHNOLOGY (402)

Self-Assessment Paper – 3

M.M. 50 **Time: 2 hrs**

General Instructions:

i. Read the question paper carefully.

ii. Question Paper is divided into four sections.

Attempt any of 10 questions from this section:

- **Section A: Multiple choice questions (1 marks each)**

Attempt any of 6 questions from this section.

- **Section B: Very short Answer (2 marks each)**

All questions are compulsory in these sections.

- **Section C: Short Answer (3 marks each)**
- **Section D: Long Answer (5 marks each)**

Section A: Multiple Choice Questions (1 marks each)

1. ____________ is used to grab the attention of the students and keep them engaged?
2. Which of the following is the count of default number of worksheets in Excel workbook?
   a. 4 b. 3
   c. 2 d. 1
3. ____________ unit carries out the basic calculations and comparison operations on the data.
4. The major pollutant for automobile exhaust is:
   a. NO b. CO
   c. SO2 d. Soot
5. What home row key does your right middle finger rest on?
   a. J b. K
   c. L d. I
6. Manufacturing of diesel generator sets is an example of green job.
   a. True b. Partially True
   c. False d. Partially False
7. Which bar is usually located below that Title Bar that provides categorized options?
   a. Menu bar b. Status Bar
   c. Toolbar d. Scroll bar

8. Which of the following is not something that can be invested?
   a. Energy b. Expertise
   c. Money d. Time
9. ___________ source is used to add the images to a presentation.
   a. Bansai b. Graffiti
   c. Shape Fill d. Clip Art
10. In verbal communication message is delivered using:
   a. Spoken or written message b. Message that uses words of any language
   c. Both a and b d. None

Section B: Very Short Questions (2 marks each)

1. What is the importance of communication channel?
2. What is the output of given equation:
   - 4 + 6 * 7
   - (5 * 7) ^ 2
3. Define Green skills?
4. Which two documents are essential for mail merge?

   Or

   Define Scrollbar? Name various types of scrollbar in MS Excel.
5. What do you mean by self-confidence?
6. Define External memory of a system?
7. Give example of clear and complete communication.
8. What are the four main sub-sectors in the IT-BPM industry?

Section C: Short Questions (3 marks each)

1. Differentiate phrase and sentence with example.
2. Explain various types of corporate business enterprises.
3. Write a short note on the relationship between man and environment.
4. Give various formulas using cell address and operators.
5. Give various types of text alignment options in detail with their shortcuts.
6. Mention any four ways of controlling water pollution.

Section D: Long Questions (5 marks each)

1. What is the functionality of data validation in Ms-Excel? How it can be applied to data series.
2. Explain the utility of page margin setup for printing the document. Also highlight the important points of custom page margin.

INFORMATION TECHNOLOGY (402)

Self-Assessment Paper – 4

M.M. 50 **Time: 2 hrs**

General Instructions:

i. Read the question paper carefully.

ii. Question Paper is divided into four sections.

Attempt any of 10 questions from this section:

- **Section A: Multiple choice questions (1 marks each)**
  Attempt any of 6 questions from this section.
- **Section B: Very short Answer (2 marks each)**
  All questions are compulsory in these sections.
- **Section C: Short Answer (3 marks each)**
- **Section D: Long Answer (5 marks each)**

Section A: Multiple Choice Questions (1 marks each)

1. Which of the following is used before the number to preserve a leading 0 in the number 03888?
   a. Full stop b. Quote
   c. Apostrophe d. Comma
2. While typing one should keep their elbow at ____________.
   a. Straight b. Right angle
   c. Curved d. Left angle
3. To insert non-adjacent columns, hold down the ____________ key while you select non-adjacent columns.
4. ____________ is the checklist consists of various elements of communication skills.
   a. 5 E's of communication b. 5 C's of communication
   c. 7 E's of communication d. 7 C's of communication
5. Thesaurus tool in MS Word is used for:
   a. Spelling suggestions b. Grammar options
   c. Synonyms and Antonyms words d. All of above
6. The ____________ is a special toolbar that displays a series of names, each of which represents a list of commands that can be used to perform tasks.
7. Soap and detergent are the source of organic pollutants like:
   a. Glycerol b. Polyphosphates
   c. Sulphonated hydrocarbons d. All of these

8. Modem stands for ___________.
   a. Modulation and demodulation
   b. Modulator and demodulator
   c. Module and demodule
   d. Memory and digital
9. Which of the following panes is not available in Task Pane?
   a. Getting Started
   b. Clip Art
   c. Word Art
   d. Search Results
10. ___________ article is used before words starting with vowels.
   a. A
   b. An
   c. The
   d. Definite article

Section B: Very Short Questions (2 marks each)

1. What do you mean by effective communication?
2. What is the meaning of manufacturing and trading based business?
3. What is the purpose of an outline view in a workspace?

   Or

   What do you call the document created in a spreadsheet application?
4. Define the usage of enter or return key?
5. What are the emerging skills in ICT?
6. My customers are not buying my food product because they do not like the flavour of it. What step of the business should I follow next?
7. Name various factors affecting perspective in communication.
8. What is the full form of the following terms:
   a. BPO
   b. BPM
   c. GDP

Section C: Short Questions (3 marks each)

1. Describe the four types of sentences with an example of each.
2. Give various factors that causes imbalance in the environment.
3. Name various existing popular spreadsheet software?
4. Give the usage of any five special keys of the computer keyboard.
5. Is it possible to select a cell, row, column or table in a slide of PowerPoint? If yes, then tell the way to do it.
6. Explain non-verbal communication along with its various elements.

Section D: Long Questions (5 marks each)

1. Define the page margin setting in excel. Differentiate between the portrait and Landscape orientation feature of excel.
2. What do you mean by desktop operating system? Give the features of DOS aswell?

INFORMATION TECHNOLOGY (402)

Self-Assessment Paper – 5

M.M. 50 **Time: 2 hrs**

General Instructions:

i. Read the question paper carefully.

ii. Question Paper is divided into four sections.

Attempt any of 10 questions from this section:

- **Section A: Multiple choice questions (1 marks each)**
  Attempt any of 6 questions from this section.
- **Section B: Very short Answer (2 marks each)**
  All questions are compulsory in these sections.
- **Section C: Short Answer (3 marks each)**
- **Section D: Long Answer (5 marks each)**

Section A: Multiple Choice Questions (1 marks each)

1. The ____________ click of a mouse often displays a list of commands on the screen.
2. What is the best way to start your day positively?
   a. Think about all that can go wrong
   b. Think about the difficult test you will face during the day
   c. Think about all your accomplishments so far and feel good about it
   d. Think about the traffic on the road and feel stressed
3. When integrating Word and Excel, word is usually the:
   a. Server b. Destination
   c. Client d. Both b. and c.
4. One way communication is ____________ due to absence of receiver response.
5. The pollution which does not persistent harm to life supporting system is:
   a. Noise pollution b. Radiation pollution
   c. Organochlorine pollution d. All of these
6. The default count of buttons present on the Quick Access Toolbar.
   a. Seven b. Six
   c. Four d. Three

7. Transactions can be done anytime, anywhere through the internet by ___________.
   a. E-commerce
   b. E-banking
   c. E-Governance
   d. None of these
8. Speed of CPU is measured in:
   a. Hertz
   b. Microhertz
   c. Megahertz
   d. Minihertz
9. The difference between Slide Design and Auto Content Wizard is:
   a. Both are same
   b. AutoContent Wizard is just the wizard version of Slide Design
   c. Slide Design does not provide sample content but Auto Content Wizard provides sample content tool
   d. Slide Design asks your choice in steps but Auto Content Wizard does not let you make choices
10. Which of the following is not a factor affecting perspective in communication?
   a. Feelings
   b. Prejudice
   c. Attitude
   d. Love

Section B: Very Short Questions (2 marks each)

1. What are the advantages and disadvantages of oral communication?
2. How resource efficiency helps in attaining the green economy?
3. What is the need of copying and moving slides?
4. What is the difference between spreadsheet, worksheet and sheet?
5. Name the various input devices of computers.

   Or

   Give the type of arrow keys on the keyboard.
6. What are presentation tools used for?
7. What do you mean by Control Unit in ALU?
8. Explain the asserted or declarative sentences with examples.

Section C: Short Questions (3 marks each)

1. What is the role of navigation tree in the Lesson editor?
2. How do you insert 4 columns in the spreadsheet.
3. Discuss few features of Wi-Fi adopter?
4. Give in brief about formatting images in slide.
5. What are prepositions? Explain it with the help of example.
6. Give various benefits of moving towards green economy?

Section D: Long Questions (5 marks each)

1. What is the purpose of Filter utility in MS-Excel? Also explain the purpose of sort in excel.
2. Explain the various referencing styles which we can apply in Ms-Word. Also highlight the insert Footnote feature.